# LEADERSHIP, NOT SALESMANSHIP:

## The Art of Leading and Serving

By
Stephen C. Morrow

xulon
PRESS

*Leadership, Not Salesmanship*
by Stephen C. Morrow

Printed in the United States of America

Library of Congress Control Number: 2002111280
ISBN 1-591602-16-5



Xulon Press
11350 Random Hills Road
Suite 800
Fairfax, VA 22030
(703) 279-6511
XulonPress.com

To order additional copies,
call 1-866-909-BOOK (2665).

# DEDICATION

**To Jean**
**Matt and Rachael**
**Brady, Missy, and Jack**

# ACKNOWLEDGMENTS

I am obliged to many for their support and cooperation, without which this book would still be a goal rather than a reality. A special word of gratitude is in order to:

My family, for whom this book is dedicated;

President, Dr. C. Pat Taylor, and the Southwest Baptist University Board of Trustees for so graciously granting me the opportunity to focus on this project;

Congressman Roy Blunt and Roseann Blunt for their encouragement and help;

My colleagues at Southwest Baptist University for hanging in there with me, especially Courtney Stalker, Ronda Middleton, Amy Welch, Rachel Hall, Julia Orrell,, Dr. Gordon Dutile, and my fellow executive cabinet officers;

The student body of Southwest Baptist University for their patience and understanding, and former student Kelli Fulton for her general assistance;

Dr. Vernon Armitage, Reverend Gary Gilmore, Vice-President for Business and Student Affairs (at a sister institution) Tom Dugger, and Attorney Amber Slayton for their kind letters of endorsement.

# TABLE OF CONTENTS

# FOREWORD

Leadership is learned. That is why I believe this book can be an invaluable primer. Leadership for the sake of service is leadership in the best sense of the word. Those who aspire to lead out of a motivation to improve the lot of others, discover a special kind of fulfillment that cannot be compared to other more tangible rewards.

If the combination of leadership and service was compelling for Americans prior to September 11, 2001, it is even more conclusive in the aftermath of the attacks on the World Trade Center and the Pentagon. Terrorists, driven by a hatred for American values, appear to have awakened scores of United States citizens to a new dawn. Out of the ashes of 9-11, a renewed sense of community is taking hold in our nation.

It has, of course, always been true of Americans. We seem to instinctively join forces whenever our most fundamental tenets are threatened. Tom Brokaw captured its essence in *The Greatest Generation.* Not only did men and women from that generation unite to win a world war, they proceeded to contribute in the second half of the twentieth century during a period of unprecedented growth and prosperity in America.

Now another generation is stepping forward in leadership and service. This book, therefore, is both timely and practical. At a time when the importance of basic values surrounding faith, family, friendship and freedom are being revisited, opportunities abound for leadership and service.

While I was President of Southwest Baptist University in the mid 1990's, I worked closely with Steve Morrow, the school's chief student life officer. I appointed Steve to this position, in part because I was convinced that he and I share a common philosophy regarding college students. As fathers of college-age sons and daughters, we maintained a realistic view of young adults. At the same time, we wanted to provide a character building atmosphere on campus that would equip students for more than a particular vocation. We reasoned that college graduates are more fully prepared for life's challenges after experiencing strong academic training with values added.

These challenges are often complex, and include some that were previously unimaginable. Still, I believe they are challenges that may be effectively addressed by the kind of leadership and service chronicled in this book.

Congressman Roy Blunt
The $7^{th}$ District of Missouri
United States House of Representatives
Washington, D.C.

# INTRODUCTION

In accepting the nomination of his party for President of the United States in July of 1960, John F. Kennedy spoke of an imminent "New Frontier." After challenging his fellow citizens "to be pioneers on that New Frontier," Kennedy proclaimed:

> My call is to the young in heart, regardless of age—to all who respond to the scriptural call: "Be strong and of a good courage; be not afraid, neither be thou dismayed."
>
> For courage—not complacency—is our need today— leadership—not salesmanship . . .[1]

As noted in the title, this is a book about leadership, not salesmanship. It is not, therefore, a business-help book. (The term "customer friendly" is nowhere to be found in the ensuing chapters.) Nor is it meant as an exhaustive work concerning all that may be involved in either the personal exercise of leadership or the provision of service to others.

Instead, this dual approach text examines leadership and service as co-existing parts of a whole concept. Moreover, it offers an account that focuses on addressing human needs as opposed to achieving personal or corporate gain. To the extent that today's leaders and would-be leaders—from various walks of life—are challenged to consider this unifying view of leadership and service, this book will have served its intended purpose.

Real life examples are interspersed throughout the book to complement the material. Some reflect first-hand knowledge and experience. Others reference well-known individuals whose professions range from politics to professional sports.

One must be familiar with the nuances of leadership per se before one is capable of providing service through leadership. Thus, Part One explores certain fundamental precepts of leadership.

Chapter one provides a basic overview, drawing clear distinctions between leadership and management. Additionally, this chapter furnishes a working definition of leadership and an explanation of its nature.

The individual leader is the subject of chapter two. What do people look for in a leader? What sets a leader apart? This chapter explores the unique role of the leader in an effort to answer these and other critical questions.

Various stages of leadership are delineated in chapters three and four. These chapters depict the unfolding aspects of leadership, from the vision of the leader to the enlistment of others in implementing that vision.

The service element is joined in Part Two, not as an afterthought but as a primary ingredient. While Part One is essential for foundational purposes, Part

Two is necessary for the sake of completeness.

Chapter five describes inherently personal characteristics associated with service. In this chapter, the idea of selflessness is presented and divided into four segments. They include self-denial (yielding), self-sacrifice (love), self-discipline (integrity), and self-deprecation (humility).

Chapter six identifies four inherent elements of service. They are empathy, encouragement, facilitation, and appreciation. Each element reflects a quality of servitude that, when enacted, translates into a pattern of personal application. In conclusion the chapter outlines a five-step utilitarian approach to service.

Perseverance is thematic in chapters seven and eight. In these closing chapters, one's potential for maintaining a sense of service is assessed in the context of personal lifestyle. The focus of these chapters is on self renewal and maintaining one's credibility in service.

A Postscript is added following the end of Part Two (immediately after chapter eight). This segment of the book encapsulates leadership and service, and includes this personal charge to lead and serve:

**L**ove both God and your neighbor...

**E**volve as a leader (it takes time)...

**A**spire to be part of something bigger than yourself...

**D**are to fail so that you may succeed...

and

**S**hare your talents and abilities—that's why God gave them to you...

**E**arn the respect of those you serve...
**R**emember that your decisions impact others...
**V**est your life in the lives of others...
**E**ntrust yourself to God...

As we begin to make our way in a twenty-first century surrounded by continuous change and uncertainty, I find a measure of reassurance in the notion that some things remain timeless. Such is the case, I believe, with respect to the linkage of leadership and service in that this connection reflects a principle rooted in scripture.

The Gospel of Mark, Chapter 10, verse 43, appears to capture its essence in these seemingly paradoxical, yet profound words of Jesus:

> "...whoever wants to become great among you must be your servant."[2]

## ENDNOTES

1. John F. Kennedy, "Address of Senator John F. Kennedy Accepting the Democratic Party Nomination for the Presidency of the United States, Memorial Coliseum, Los Angeles, July 15, 1960." Home Page. 26 December 2001 <http://www.cs.umb.edu/jfklibrary/j071560.htm>

2. Quotation is taken from *New International Version Disciple's Study Bible* (Nashville: Holman Bible Publishers, 1988), 1247.

# PART ONE: LEADERSHIP

## Chapter One:

# GRASPING THE CONCEPT OF LEADERSHIP

**"Leadership is a serving relationship that has the effect of facilitating human development."**
**Ted Ward**

Several years ago a popular soft drink was marketed to the public by way of a catchy commercial spot that proclaimed "it's so misunderstood." Translation: Judge our product by its taste, not its name.

Similarly, the concept of leadership is sometimes misunderstood. For example, leadership and management are often viewed in the same vein. The two terms, however, are not synonymous. Retired U.S. Navy Admiral Grace Murray Hopper has said it most succinctly: "You manage things; you lead people."[1]

Leadership requires a forward-looking mentality, while management revolves around more immediate circumstances in which pressing matters often seem to take on a life of their own. Furthermore, leadership involves broad strokes that help foster a conception of the big picture. Management, on the other hand, is a more precise practice that tends to zero in on such areas as personnel policies, lines of authority, and work flow. The upshot is that leadership is less concerned with making the trains run on time than it is with lofty ideals and transforming those ideals into reality.

This is not to suggest that the functions of day-to-day administration (management) are somehow less significant than leadership performance. On the contrary, efficient management goes a long way toward ensuring the success of any operation. Still, the fact remains that even a highly competent manager does not necessarily translate into an effective leader, and an able leader may or may not be a skillful manager.

The following list includes a further rendering of differences between management and leadership roles:

Managers make sure that things work well. Leaders create that which works better.

Managers solve today's problems. Leaders create a better future.

Managers focus on the process. Leaders focus on the product.

Managers make sure the details are taken

care of. Leaders set broad purposes and directions.

Managers make sure that people put in an honest day's work for an honest day's pay and that they are rewarded for doing so. Leaders inspire people to do more than expected.

Managers organize and plan to meet this year's objectives. Leaders create a vision of the organization several years hence.

Managers create efficient policies and standard operating procedures. Leaders go beyond standard procedures and create a more effective system.

Managers focus on efficiency. Leaders focus on effectiveness.

Managers focus on problem behavior and seek to improve it through counseling, coaching, and nurturing. Leaders focus on what is going right and praise it.

Managers worry about the present. Leaders look forward to the future.[2]

As we have observed, leadership may be misconstrued for that which it is not. It is also susceptible to a fragmentary understanding of its nature. Some, for example, will readily identify themselves with the notion of leadership and its merits, only to quickly disassociate themselves from the very thought of any kind of political activity (behavior they would openly disdain).

Here, however, is a news flash! Like it or not, effective leadership inevitably requires some degree of political prowess. Even leadership for the sole purpose of meeting the needs of others cannot escape the hard reality of politics.

In 1996 Roy Blunt (see Foreword) made the decision to re-enter the political arena. (Roy had served as Missouri's Secretary of State for eight years prior to accepting a University Presidency in 1992.) When asked how he would be able to balance the early stages of a congressional campaign with his duties as CEO for an institution of higher education, Roy's response was both humorous and insightful. "That won't be a problem," he said. "When things get too political, I'll just get away from my office at the university and return to the campaign trail." Successful in his bid to become a member of the United States House of Representatives, Congressman Blunt realized that he had essentially moved from one political environment to another.

Nationally syndicated columnist and talk show host, Chris Matthews, provides this perspective on the intrinsic role of politics in everyday life.

> How many times have you heard a colleague complain that he failed to get a promotion because of "office politics?" Or someone say that she turned her back on an opportunity because she "couldn't hack all of the favoritism?" What about the "backstabbing and sharks" who haunt the corridors of business and professional

> power? But we all know people who have succeeded swiftly and magnificently while others plod along one yard and a cloud of dust at a time. The fact is, there's a great deal of politics in everyday life...
>
> In every field of endeavor there are people who could easily be successful but who spend their entire lives making one political mistake after another. They become so absorbed in themselves that they ignore the very people they would most like to influence. Rather than recruit allies, they limit their horizons to missions they can accomplish alone. Instead of confronting or seducing their adversaries, they avoid them. In making important deals, they become obsessed with intangibles and give away the store. They become crippled by handicaps when they could be exploiting them.
>
> Some might say these tendencies are only human. But such tendencies that pass for human nature, our hesitancy to ask for things, our unease in the face of opposition, are instincts for accommodation rather than leadership...[3]

Now that we have discerned that leadership is not management, and have recognized that leadership is not immune from politics, we are ready to grapple with this fundamental question: What, then, is leadership?

In basic terms, leadership is "the ability to influence others to follow."[4] Dr. John C. Maxwell is even more to the point in this concise definition:

> Leadership is influence. This is my straightforward definition of leadership. It's a simple, straightforward one word description that places leadership within everyone's reach. All of us can exercise a certain degree of influence on someone, at some point, in some place. Leadership isn't about titles, positions, or flow charts. It's about one life influencing another.[5]

A similar, but somewhat more substantive definition comes from Dr. William A. Cohen, a retired Major General in the United States Air Force Reserves who has seen combat duty in both the American and Israeli Air Forces. Dr. Cohen, who has leadership experience in business and education as well as the military and other organizations, is a fellow-believer in the idea that leadership is largely the ability to exercise influence over others.

> Let me propose a definition of leadership to you. With this definition, it doesn't make any difference whether you are leading a company, an organization, a military unit, or just some friends in a club. Leadership is the art of influencing others to their maximum performance to accomplish any task, objective, or project.[6]

A fuller grasp of leadership requires an appreciation for that which is at its core. As observed in the aforementioned definitions, influence appears central in leadership. Let us, therefore, briefly explore this intimation.

Influence is typically associated with position (one's base of operation). Therein lie two contrasting images.

The first image envisions position as a vehicle for control. Power is the common denominator in this equation.

**POSITION + INFLUENCE BASED ON POWER = CONTROL**

While power alone has the capacity to produce results, it is not without its drawbacks. For example, some in positions of leadership may be prone to use power for self-serving purposes, or simply as a demonstration of their authority. In either case, this kind of application would seem likely to bring forth an image more akin to raw power and intimidation, than the practice of leadership.

The late Richard Nixon, thirty-seventh President of the United States, included a chapter on power in a book he authored after leaving office. In referring to his predecessor, Nixon had this to say:

> When I saw an embittered Lyndon Johnson after he left the White House, he told me, "People don't support you because they like you. You can count on a person's support only when you can do something for him or something to him."[7]

While it cannot be denied that an element of truth is present in Johnson's words, we should ponder whether this represents a statement on leadership or control. A capacity exists, I believe, that would call us to a higher plane in our understanding of leadership and all that it entails.

This brings us to a second contrasting image, one that fuses position with character. In this instance, the equation requires an adjustment.

**POSITION + INFLUENCE BASED ON CHARACTER = LEADERSHIP**

If the first image reflects a picture of arrogance, the second mirrors a portrait of servitude in which followers are drawn, not out of a sense of coercion, but as a result of favorable characteristics associated with the leader (a notion more completely addressed in Chapter Two). At this point, let it suffice to state that leadership is not simply the practice of running roughshod over people to get things done. Nor is leadership serving others in order to exercise influence over them. Rather, leadership invites influence as a result of serving human needs and cultivating human development.

One early June morning a few years ago, I was working quietly at my desk in the Office of Student Life. I was attempting to catch up on some paper-work-while the students were home between semesters-when I glanced up and noticed I had a visitor. One of our international students, a young lady from Australia, was standing in the doorway. "Hi, Alison. What can I do for you?" I asked. In her unmistakable down under accent she replied, "Mr. Morrow, I'm boahed" (sic). "You're what?" I inquired. "Boahed, I'm boahed," she repeated. "Oh, you are bored," I said, quickly realizing that she was still living on campus while all of her friends had gone home for the summer.

It seems that Alison had attempted to check out a novel from the university library, only to be rejected because her card would not register. (Since we were between semesters, she was technically not enrolled in school at that moment.) As I walked with her to the library to see if I could help with this little problem, I found myself thinking how difficult it must be for her to go about her business in a country other than her own. (She told me that even the fast food restaurants were forever confusing her order at the drive-thru due to her accent.)

As luck would have it, when we arrived at the front desk a brand new employee (whom I had not met) was on the job. "Excuse me," I said. "Is there anything we can do to get this young lady a library book? If necessary, I will be glad to check one out for her on my employee card." The woman's response was quick and to the point. "Are you a teacher here?" Trying my best to avoid a condescending tone, I very nonchalantly informed her that I was a vice president. "Oh," she exclaimed. "Well I am sure there is something we can do to take care of this." At that point, Alison saved the day by interjecting the comment, "Mr. Morrow teaches life."

Not only had Alison helped both the lady at the front desk and me recover from our rather awkward exchange, she had said something I will never forget. Whether or not true in my own case, Alison's words struck a chord. What more appropriate words could be uttered, with respect to anyone who would lead and serve, than he or she teaches life?

A more compelling story is told by Mitch

Albom. In the 1970's Mitch was a student at Brandeis University in Waltham, Massachusetts. His favorite teacher was Morrie Schwartz, a professor of behavioral science. The following synopsis sets the stage for that which would come later.

> It is the late spring of 1979, a hot, sticky Saturday afternoon. Hundreds of us sit together side by side, in rows of wooden folding chairs on the main campus lawn. We wear blue nylon robes. We listen impatiently to long speeches. When the ceremony is over, we throw our caps in the air, and we are officially graduated from college, the senior class of Brandeis University in the city Waltham, Massachusetts. For many of us, the curtain has just come down on childhood.
>
> Afterward, I find Morrie Schwartz, my favorite professor, and introduce him to my parents...He tells my parents how I took every class he taught. He tells them, "You have a special boy here." Embarrassed, I look at my feet. Before we leave, I hand my professor a present, a tan briefcase with his initials on the front. I bought this the day before at the shopping mall. I didn't want to forget him. Maybe I didn't want him to forget me...[8]

Fast forward to 1995. Mitch Albom has learned that his former professor, now in his seventies, is dying of amyotrophic lateral sclerosis, better known as Lou Gehrig's disease. In an extraordinary sequence of events, after failing to stay in touch since his college graduation day, Mitch travels from out of state to Morrie's home. The two reunite and Mitch returns for regular visits during the final months of Morrie's life. It is the last class Mitch would take with his favorite professor, and it includes some of the best lessons. For example:

> "There's a big confusion in this country over what we want versus what we need," said Morrie. "You need food, you want a chocolate sundae...You know what really gives you satisfaction?" What? "Offering others what you have to give...Devote yourself to loving others, devote yourself to your community around you, and devote yourself to creating something that gives you purpose and meaning."[9]

Thus, leadership is about the ability to successfully pour one's life into the lives of others in such a manner that it will spur them to service as well. In this regard, leadership involves influence not just <u>over</u> others, but on behalf of others. It is the kind of leadership that can be exerted from one's personal or professional base in life.

Former President George Bush (affectionately known as "number 41" in family circles) seems to subscribe to this view of leadership. Referring to power as a base—as opposed to a means for control—the former President's words speak for themselves:

> Use power to help people. For we are given power not to advance our own pur-

> poses, nor to make a great show in the world, nor a name. There is but one just use of power, and it is to serve people.[10]

We live in a time in which terms are often tossed around lightly and intermingled in order to make a point. At the risk of being guilty of such a practice, I am convinced that the kind of power alluded to by the first President Bush is well illustrated by the earthly life of Jesus Christ. While He preached humility, His power was apparent to those who were drawn to Him. The less fortunate in life were not magnetically attracted to Him because they realized who He was in a spiritual sense. Even His disciples struggled off and on with that question. Instead, the poor, the weak, the sick, and even the children, seemed to sense His singular capacity for translating power into the betterment of human lives. Present day leaders would, I believe, be well-advised to learn from this example.

Regardless of how much power today's leaders may have at their disposal, after all is said and done leadership remains a learned art. As such, it has potential for development in a number of settings.

Politicians, members of the media, business men and women, educators, ministers, coaches and athletes, military personnel, professional entertainers, and those engaged in public and private service endeavors are candidates for leadership. While leadership is typically thought of in the context of the workplace, its boundaries are limitless. Students, for example, have opportunities to become involved in leadership at school, as do members of faith-based congregations in their places of worship. The family unit and the community at large offer further possibilities.

Notwithstanding the leadership opportunities that may be present in various environments, it is important to keep in mind that people in positions of leadership do not always execute leadership. True leadership (or the lack thereof) hinges on the ability and determination of those who step forward to lead.

## ITEMS FOR DISCUSSION

1. Identify and discuss a distinction drawn between management and leadership.
2. Explain the role of politics in leadership.
3. Explain the distinctions between the two equations presented in this chapter.
4. Identify and discuss job-related environments where leadership may take place.
5. Identify and discuss environments (other than work environments) where leadership may take place.

## ENDNOTES

1. Excerpts taken from: John C. Maxwell, *Leadership 101—Inspirational Quotes & Insights For Leaders* (Tulsa, Oklahoma: Honor Books, 1997), 16. Used by permission of Honor Boods, Tulsa, Oklahoma. All rights reserved.

2. Rick Lynch and Sue Vineyard, *Secrets of Leadership* (Downers Grove, Illinois: Heritage Arts Publishing, 1991), 6.

3. Chris Matthews, *Hardball* (New York: Touch Stone, 1998),

Copyright 16-18. Excerpts reprinted with permission of Simon & Schuster Adult Publishing Group.

4. Lynch and Vineyard, *Secrets of Leadership*, 2.

5. Maxwell, *Leadership 101—Inspirational Quotes & Insights For Leaders*, 4-5.

6. William A. Cohen, *The New Art of The Leader* (Paramus, New Jersey: Prentice Hall, 2000), 12.

7. Richard M. Nixon, *In The Arena—A Memoir of Victory, Defeat, and Renewal* (New York: Simon and Schuster, 1990), 207.

8. Mitch Albom, *Tuesdays With Morrie—An Old Man, A Young Man, And Life's Greatest Lessons* (New York: Doubleday, 1997), 3-4.

9. Albom, *Tuesdays With Morrie—An Old Man, A Young Man, And Life's Greatest Lessons*, 126-127.

10. Maxwell, *Leadership 101—Inspirational Quotes & Insights For Leaders*, 8.

# Chapter Two:

# THE LEADER

**"A Leader is a dealer in hope"**
**Napoleon Bonaparte**

Having analyzed leadership in conceptual terms, let us shift our thoughts to the individual leader. What defines a leader? Moreover (and in a much more practical sense), what do people look for in a leader? Finally, what qualities can be precisely identified that appear to set a leader apart from those who would follow?

A leader is a person of influence who possesses a knowledge of what needs to be done and the ability to get it done. An effective leader may be further defined as one who holds a set of core convictions and is able to implement those beliefs by means of pragmatic decision making. Unlike one who functions strictly as an accommodator, a leader is not driven by pragmatic instincts. Still, a leader must be able to recognize when and how to be flexible.

Although the aforementioned thoughts are

descriptive of a leader, they are not necessarily indicative of what people actually look for in a leader. Strip away the rhetoric, and we are left with this basic longing: what we desire in a leader is someone with the capacity to instill in us an anticipation of a future that will improve upon our past or present set of circumstances. In short, we want a leader who will inspire a level of consciousness concerning that which may be.

I have never been a Jesse Jackson loyalist. However, I am convinced that Reverend Jackson is on to something when he encourages his followers to "keep hope alive." A good leader, I believe, will do just that, even in the midst of trying circumstances.

Much has been written about the ability of President Franklin Delano Roosevelt to maintain hope among the American people during the ominous years of the Great Depression and World War II. A part from his New Deal economic programs and his skills in international statesmanship, FDR seemed to possess a kind of self-confidence and optimism that came through to both the public at large and those within his personal sphere of influence.

> No factor was more important to Roosevelt's leadership than his confidence in himself and the American people. "His most outstanding characteristic is an air of supreme self-confidence," journalist W.M. Kiplinger wrote as the crisis of the European War deepened. "He always gives the impression that to him nothing is impossible, that everything will turn out all right."

> The President had a remarkable capacity to transmit this cheerful strength to others, to allow, White House Counsel Sam Rosenman observed, "those who hear it to begin to feel it and to return it tenfold by their own confidence." Francis Perkins claimed that his capacity to inspire and encourage those who had to do tough, confused and practically impossible jobs was beyond dispute. Like everyone else, she said, she "came away from an interview with the President feeling better, not because he had solved any problems...but because he had made me more cheerful, stronger, more determined."[1]

If Roosevelt's forte was cultivating a sense of hope, such was also the case regarding President Ronald Reagan. And while both men were effective communicators, what they had to say was at least as important as how they said it. Like FDR, Reagan came to power at a time of sinking expectations. His long time aide, Michael Deaver, had this to say with respect to his former boss:

> I firmly believe that God watches out for this world in which we live. Maybe He's a little biased toward the United States, because the right people just seem to come along when they are needed most.
>
> In 1980, Americans were under siege, afflicted with a "malaise" that was tightening its grip in the form of long gas lines, insufferable inflation, and a dwindling

> national pride. Twenty- and thirty somethings can't know what waited for Reagan when he stepped into office in January 1981. Hostages in Iran, Soviets on the move in Central America and the Middle East, an economy in the tank, the U.S. military flat on its back, relentless foreign competition bruising our greatest companies. The American flag was an object of scorn overseas. We were on the verge of becoming a laughing stock.
>
> Americans were rightly beginning to doubt themselves, but a man came along who knew the true score. He knew that better times were ahead because "after all, we're Americans." The nation cried out, and a guy named Ron answered the call. He resuscitated not only the diminished office of the President, but the national pride that had lain dormant since the early 1960s. Clearly, Reagan was the right man at the right timc, and history will bear his name triumphantly.[2]

In addition to wanting leaders who offer hope for the future, my observation is that people tend to respond best to leaders who are at ease with themselves. Again, Ronald Reagan serves as a case-in-point. Rather than attempting to be someone or something he was not, Reagan was quite content to simply maximize who he was. In so doing, he was able to embody an important trait, one that plays a key role in setting a leader apart. Again, Michael

Deaver explains:

> What's the secret of Ronald Reagan's immense success? The guy knows who he is. In the public relations business I constantly tell clients—corporations or candidates, it doesn't matter—if you don't know who you are, there's not a lot I can do for you. My first realization of how comfortable Reagan was in his own skin came during the late 1960s. We were staying at the Waldorf Astoria Hotel in New York City, where the governor had given a speech. The next morning I received a call from him. "Let's go for a walk," he said.
>
> I met him in the lobby fifteen minutes later and we strolled out onto the sidewalk. I could tell Reagan was feeling chipper by the look on his face and the spring in his step. Within about ten minutes or so, a middle-aged fellow approached us with a beaming smile. "Hey, I know you from television, and you're the best. You're Ray Milland!"
>
> Without embarrassment, Reagan looked down toward the sidewalk and grinned as the man shoved a pen and paper into his chest, seeking an autograph. Reagan obligingly signed it "Ray Milland." The man walked away happy as a clam.
>
> "Why did you do that?" I said. "You're the governor of California. Why didn't you tell him?"

> "Mike," he said softly, "I know who I am. Don't ever worry about me."
>
> I would have plenty of cause to worry about Reagan in the decades ahead—cause even to fear for him—but about his sense of self, his understanding of who and what he was, I would never again fret. Lots of people in politics are someone else's man; that's the nature of the beast. But Ronald Reagan belonged to no one else. He believed in bedrock values: honesty, humility, and integrity may be first among them. And he never aspired to be anyone or anything other than himself. In fact, when I think back over the twenty years that I worked for Reagan, and the countless people who came in and out of his life, the only one who didn't change was Reagan.[3]

A discussion of world leaders gives rise to an age-old question. Are leaders defined by events, or do leaders shape events?

Some, for example, contend that Winston Churchill would be remembered as little more than a footnote in history but for the occurrence of World War II and Churchill's subsequent leadership role. Was Churchill a great leader, or was his leadership magnified as a result of his words and actions during those dark years? In this case, at least, perhaps the answer is yes and yes.

And if events contribute favorably to one's perceived effectiveness as a leader, cannot the reverse be true as well? President Richard Nixon would no doubt be primarily remembered for his foreign policy successes, but for the Watergate scandal that brought down his presidency. With Americans held hostage in Iran and a sour economy at home, President Jimmy Carter was given a vote of no confidence by the American people in 1980. (As a result of admirable service since leaving office, Carter's image now appears somewhat restored.) President Bill Clinton presided over a robust national economy. But it is probably safe to suggest that average Americans are more likely to remember the name of a certain White House intern than that of any high ranking economic official during the Clinton years.

Finally, what may be said about the leadership of President George W. Bush? On September 10, 2001, Bush had been President of the United States for two-hundred and thirty-four days. By most accounts he was still trying to find his way clear of the lingering clouds from the November (and December) 2000 election results. He unwittingly did so in the weeks and months that followed the September 11$^{th}$ terrorist attacks on America. No longer viewed simply as his father's son, Bush and his leadership ability will now be defined by his response to a national tragedy, a reality he seemed to instinctively comprehend. In finding his stride, he seemed to speak not with eloquence, but resolve. And his actions appeared propelled not by contempt, but a sense of determination.

It is useful, I believe, for leaders and potential leaders to consider recognizable traits associated with high profile public figures (both past and present). The reasoning is simple. Leadership qualities have universal applicability.

Jim Kouzes and Barry Posner are respected authorities on the subject of leadership. In a 1995 study they found the most admired characteristics of a leader include these four qualities that stand out above others:[4]

| Characteristics | % of people selecting |
|---|---|
| Honest | 88 |
| Forward-looking | 75 |
| Inspiring | 68 |
| Competent | 63 |

Notwithstanding the unquestionable merit of scientific research, and the benefit of learning from others, one must ultimately look inward to come to grips with one's personal capacity for leadership. And, as noted, knowing oneself and being comfortable in that knowledge can be advantageous.

One way this can be accomplished is by engaging in an introspective question and answer time with oneself. For this session to serve its intended purpose, one must be as forthright as possible in answering questions such as:

1. What fundamental values do I hold dear? (It may be helpful to break these down into categories.)
    a. Personal spiritual values
    b. Ethical values
    c. Family values

   d. Values related to education and career
   e. Political values (See Appendix A for an instrument designed to measure political values.)
   f. Values related to leisure and entertainment
   g. Relationship values—friends and acquaintances
   h. Community oriented values—local, state, and national
2. What are my everyday priorities?
3. What is my passion in life?
4. What are my strengths and weaknesses?
5. What are my pet peeves?

Honest answers to self-scrutinizing questions can go a long way in the search for the leader within. (Various proven psychological instruments offer additional discovery methods –The Keirsey Temperamental Sorter and The Myers-Briggs Personality Test are two prominent examples.)

Questions that directly address leadership may also be asked of oneself. These questions serve a dual purpose. First, they help personalize what leadership is all about. Second, they again necessitate an introspective examination that results in a self-assessment of leadership skills.

1. **Do I consider myself a take-charge type of person, one who is up to the task of setting the agenda?** The point is not that one always has to be in charge. Instead, the gist of this question is to help determine willingness or reluctance when it comes to stepping forward in leadership.

2. **Am I decisive, one who is not afraid to act?** Let's face it, some people don't like to be put on the spot for fear of either making a mistake or alienating someone. Still others can't quite seem to get out of the starting block. Interestingly, after they prove their capability to themselves, they are sometimes (not always) just fine. I remember when my son, Matt, first started playing little league baseball he would typically either walk or be called out on strikes when it was his turn to bat. One day I casually said to him "You know, Matty, you will never get a hit unless you swing the bat." He must have taken my words seriously because it wasn't long before he was spraying base hits all over the field. By the time he finished his senior year, he had been chosen Most Valuable Player on his high school team.
3. **When making decisions, am I able to balance firmness and flexibility?** This question concerns personal conviction and one's grasp of when and how to be pragmatic.
4. **Am I able to project self-confidence without also asserting a "my way or the highway" attitude?** There is a fine line between a healthy dose of self-confidence and an over-dose of self-will.
5. **Am I able to exercise authority without taking myself too seriously?** Someone who just tries to be a buddy to his or her followers is no real leader. On the other hand, peo-

ple in positions of authority sometimes need to learn how to "lighten-up" (or "chill" as I think the saying now goes).

6. **Am I able to avoid being disingenuous with those who are expected to follow my lead?** Nothing is more harmful to one's credibility than to say one thing to a particular individual (often in order to appease that person), only to turn around and give a different account to someone else. The strange thing is that it seems to work (at least for awhile) for some people. Eventually, however, it comes full circle.
7. **Am I more concerned with immediate circumstances or eventual outcomes?** This question is primarily directed toward one's ability to see the big picture.
8. **Do I believe that character counts in leadership?** The eventual answer to this question (as opposed to the quick "yes" answer) will separate the control-oriented persons in leadership positions from the true leaders.
9. **Am I willing to take a stand, even at the risk of criticism?** I have a poem that hangs on the wall in my office. This verse has found its way into the hearts of presidents and other leaders during times of crisis when second-guessing seems to flourish.

    Bullfight critics row on row
    Crowd the enormous plaza full,
    But only one is there who knows,
    And he is the one who fights the bull.[5]

10. **Finally, do I have what it takes to make my followers feel good about themselves?** Followers should be made to feel important, as demonstrated in this next example.

Well before baseball great Ozzie Smith had been voted into the Hall of Fame in January of 2002, his former manager, Whitey Herzog (himself a recognized leader in the world of baseball), knew that Smith was more than an outstanding player. Said Herzog: "The thing I have come to understand about Ozzie is that not only is he the greatest defensive shortstop ever to play the game, but he's also a first-rate human being, a leader in the best sense of the word."[6]

I learned the truth of that statement first hand one cold January afternoon in 1985. Accompanied by my twelve year old son, Matt, and my nine year old daughter, Missy, I found myself standing in a very long line at a shopping mall in Springfield, Missouri. The people in line were not waiting to make a purchase. They were there to get the autographs of several players from the St. Louis Cardinals who were dutifully signing away while sitting at a front table.

A month earlier, Christmas 1984, Missy had excitedly discovered that one of her Christmas gifts that year was a cabbage patch doll. (As difficult as it was to secure the much in demand doll, it's a good thing she showed some excitement!) Cabbage patch dolls came with their own names. Missy's doll was named Osmund. Immediately she announced, "I'm going to call him Ozzie, after Ozzie Smith."

Now, back to the long line at the shopping mall. After waiting for hours, I was getting tired. When we finally arrived at the table, it was apparent that the players had pretty much had their fill for the day as well. Not that they were rude. Let's just say a sense of tediousness had clearly set in. Then, all of a sudden, my two kids and I were standing before Ozzie Smith, the "Wizard of Oz!" "I named my cabbage patch doll after you," Missy proudly proclaimed, her head bobbing while her blond pig tails followed suit. As long as I live, I will never forget what happened next. Although he had to be at least as weary as the others sitting at the table, the future hall of famer drew himself up and treated my little girl like she was royalty (which, of course, to me she was—and still is). His eyes lit up as he spoke. "You did? Well, I am truly honored," he said as he made sure everyone around the table, players and fans alike, became a part of the special moment.

I learned something from that experience. As a leader, *who* you are is sometimes more revealing than *what* you are.

In this era of home run feats, I am sure that Barry Bonds and Mark McGwire are also fine individuals.

But to this day, when I walk into Busch Stadium in St. Louis to enjoy a ball game, and as I observe the countless numbers of shirts with "McGwire, 25" printed on the backs, I still wear my shirt that reads "O. Smith, 1."

## ITEMS FOR DISCUSSION

1. Explain the definition of a leader in contrast to what people actually look for in a leader.
2. Discuss a common leadership trait associated with Presidents Franklin Roosevelt and Ronald Reagan.
3. Explain why it is important for a leader to have a sense of self.
4. According to the findings of Kouzes and Posner, what four characteristics are most admired in a leader? Discuss how the four qualities may interact.
5. Identify and explain a self-imposed question specifically pertaining to one's capacity to exercise leadership skills.

## ENDNOTES

1. Doris Kearns Goodwin, *No Ordinary Time–Franklin and Eleanor Roosevelt: The Home Front in World War II* (New York: Simon & Schuster, 1994), 46. Reprinted with the permission of Simon & Schuster.

2. Michael K. Deaver, *A Different Drummer–My Thirty Years with Ronald Reagan* (New York: Harper Collins Publishers, Inc., 2001), 123.

3. Deaver, *A Different Drummer–My Thirty Years with Ronald Reagan*, 157-158.

4. Jim Kouzes and Barry Posner, *The Leadership Challenge* (San Francisco: Jossey-Bass, 1995), 21. Reprinted by permission of John Wiley & Sons, Inc.

5. Kenneth P. O'Donnell and David F. Powers with Joe McCarthy, *"Johnny, We Hardly Knew Ye" Memories of John Fitzgerald Kennedy* (Boston: Little, Brown and Company, 1970, 1972), 316.

6. Whitey Herzog and Kevin Horrigan, *White Rat–A Life in Baseball* (New York: Harper & Row, 1987), 137, by permission of the authors.

# Chapter Three:

# THE VISION

**"We all live under the same sky, but we don't have the same horizon."**
**Konrad Adenauer**

Vision has played an ever-present role in the history of humankind. At times the role has been filled by individuals with dark motives and unspeakable intentions. (Adolf Hitler and, more recently, Osama bin Laden come to mind.) At other times persons of vision have pointed the way to a bright new dawn.

In this chapter, we consider the leader as a person of well-founded vision. Attention is also given to various origins of vision. Additionally, this chapter takes into account the noble vision, the workable vision, and the natural tension that exists between the two (idealism vs practicality).

The leader bears responsibility for presenting a vision that will appeal to his or her followers. Accordingly, it is crucial that the leader first be mindful of something that Dr. John Maxwell calls "The Law of Buy In."

> When I teach leadership seminars, I field a lot of questions about vision. Invariably someone will come up to me during a break, give me a brief description of an evolving vision, and ask me "Do you think my people will buy into my vision?" My response is always the same: "First tell me this. Do your people buy into you?"
>
> You see, many people who approach the area of vision in leadership have it all backward. They believe that if the cause is good enough, people will automatically buy into it and follow. But that's not how leadership really works. People don't at first follow worthy causes. They follow worthy leaders who promote worthwhile causes. People buy into the leader first, then the leader's vision. Having an understanding of that changes your whole approach to leading people.
>
> For the person who attends one of my conferences and asks whether his people will follow, the question really becomes, "Have I given my people reasons to buy into me?" If the answer is yes, they will gladly buy into his vision. But if he has not built his credibility with his people, it really doesn't matter how great a vision he has.[1]

If it is true that people buy into the leader before they are ready to subscribe to his or her vision, the logical next question for the leader is this: What qualities must I demonstrate for people to buy into me? To avoid redundancy at this point, I will simply reference other chapters in this book as a source for answers to the previous question. (Chapter Two is particularly pertinent.)

After fulfilling Maxwell's "Law of Buy In," the leader should be primed to bring forth a vision rooted in an idea, an ideal, a conviction, a personal circumstance, or even a dream. While these origins may at times overlap, they will be considered separately.

## VISION ROOTED IN AN IDEA

According to Florence Scovel Shinn, there are three "departments of the mind." They include the "subconscious, conscious, and superconscious."

> ...The *superconscious* mind is the God mind within each man, and is the realm of perfect ideas.
>
> In it, is the *"perfect pattern"* spoken of by Plato, *The Devine Design;* for there is a *Devine Design* for each person. *"There is a place that you are to fill and no one else can fill, something you are to do, which no one else can do."* There is a perfect picture of this in the *superconscious mind.* It usually flashes across the conscious as an unattainable ideal–"something too good to be true."
>
> In reality, it is man's true destiny (or destination) flashed to him from the infi-

nite intelligence which is within himself.[2]

I do not believe that this characterization of the "superconscious" mind is meant to convey that any one of us is irreplaceable. For example, an individual who vacates his or her job may find that the replacement is able to do the work as well or perhaps better. However, the replacement will not operate in the exact manner as did his or her predecessor. Thus, it is appropriate to ask what can I bring to this position that is unique unto me? More precisely, what *ideas* do I have to offer that someone else would not entertain?

Seith Leibson is Director of Policy for Empower America. In March of 2002 I had the opportunity to interview Mr. Liebson regarding the ideas associated with this reputable national organization headquartered in Washington, D.C.

According to Liebson, Empower America was initially an idea for providing a conservative balance to the incoming Clinton Administration in 1993. The idea, he said, was to "propagate policies and propose alternative answers to White House initiatives regarding economic growth, inner city development, cultural renewal, and education reform." As part of the "loyal opposition," the plan was to work with the administration when possible and to otherwise pose separate solutions for "the least among us."

For example, one idea that has propelled Empower America from its inception is that government should not be viewed primarily in the context of giving handouts. Instead, Liebson used the analogy of a trampoline when describing the emphasis of

Empower America. "A trampoline gives you a jump," he said. By getting a jump start, Leibson said people can pursue the opportunity to control their own destiny rather than depending on government. Former Congressman and Republican nominee for Vice President in 1996, Jack Kemp, is affiliated with Empower America. Leibson mentioned that Kemp is a strong advocate of the trampoline analogy. Kemp is fond of saying "When you own something you are more apt to take care of it."

Now that the Clinton years have come and gone, Empower America is working to promote a civic agenda for America that is consistent with the priorities outlined by President Bush in his 2002 State of the Union address. With education reform already signed into law, Kemp will focus on economic progress while another high profile leader, Bill Bennett, will identify with patriotism and winning the war on terrorism. Bennett will continue to identify with cultural issues as well.

I am glad to share the gist of this interview in order to point out the power of an idea. It is an idea whose time had come in 1993, and it has attached itself to a vision that continues to make a difference in the early years of the twenty-first century.

## VISION ROOTED IN AN IDEAL

An ideal tends to be broader in scope than a specific idea. Moreover, an ideal represents the best in all of us, notwithstanding individual differences that may exist regarding specific details.

I grew up during a time of great social change in

America. In the 1960s my generation became fixated on a number of ideals including the peace movement (for those who believed that the war in Vietnam was unjust) and the civil rights movement. In many ways I am proud to be associated with the baby boomer generation. In other ways I am not. For example, I have always found it inconsistent that so many of the same people who took a stand on the great moral issues of the day, saw nothing immoral about smoking pot or tripping out on LSD.

Bill O'Reilly, the well-known host of Fox News Channel's "O'Reilly Factor," speaks for myself and others in sharing his personal thoughts on a leader from that era.

> He was the toughest politician I ever saw. He said that he never forgot a friend or an enemy, and I believe him. He took on the mob and corrupt unions. Biographers say he was "ruthless," but there's no question that Bobby Kennedy was also ruthlessly *effective*: He did what all politicians should be doing: He tried to right wrongs...[3]

Robert Kennedy was many things to many people. Some perceived him favorably, others did not. But few can doubt that he was a leader driven by ideals. His words, long since spoken, continue to echo:

> Each time a man stands up for an ideal or acts to improve the lot of others, or strikes out against injustice, he sends forth a tiny ripple of hope, and crossing each other from a million different centers of energy and daring, those ripples build a

> current that can sweep down the mightiest walls of oppression and resistance.[4]

## VISION ROOTED IN CONVICTION

Conviction differs from an idea and an ideal in at least two respects. First, it stems from a belief that something must be done. Second, there is usually a strong sense of time urgency.

In the early 1960s, the United States was engaged in a space race with the Soviet Union. It was a race in which the U.S. had fallen woefully behind. Many were worried about serious implications for America if the U.S. space program continued to lag behind that of a strong Communist regime.

On May 25, 1961, after having been briefed on the chances for success, President John F. Kennedy went before Congress to announce his bold vision for catching and by-passing the Soviets. Given Kennedy's conviction that the U.S. could not afford to trail the Soviet Union at that critical moment in history, his words were both visionary and prophetic.

> ...I believe that this nation should commit itself to achieving the goal—before this decade is out—of landing a man on the Moon and returning him safely to the Earth. No single space project in this period will be more impressive to mankind...[5]

In July of 1969, some six years and eight months after his death, Kennedy's vision was realized. Apollo II landed its crew on the surface of the Moon and returned them safely to the Earth. A visionary's conviction had become a reality.

I have noticed a couple of things regarding effective leaders whose vision is rooted in conviction. They are typically a few steps ahead of others, and they recognize that others may or may not share their conviction.

First, a visionary is able to see down the road. If the leader is going to provide a vision for the future, he or she must stay ahead of the curve.

Second, leaders with a conviction-centered vision must accept the reality that others may not instantly identify with their conviction. Some critics bear a strange resemblance to the animal characters in the story of the Little Red Hen. None of the animals wanted to help bake the bread, but all were more than willing to help eat it. I have observed that fact many times in real life. People who are initially apathetic or opposed to new facilities, new programs, or even new approaches to existing programs, are sometimes quick to enjoy the product of another individual's vision. If the vision is right, the visionary will be undeterred.

Perhaps this is an appropriate time to reiterate the relevance of Maxwell's "Law of Buy In." To get others to buy into one's vision, one must first get others to buy into him or her.[6]

## VISION ROOTED IN A PERSONAL CIRCUMSTANCE

It is not uncommon for people to develop a vision (which soon becomes a cause) as a result of a personal circumstance they are facing. Two that come to mind are gender equity-in relation to school sponsored athletic programs-and accessability for the physically challenged. However, no personal circumstance is comparable to that which results from the tragic loss of human life.

Darrell Scott is the father of Rachel Scott, one of the students who was murdered during the horrific shooting spree at Columbine High School on the outskirts of Denver, Colorado. As a parent, Mr. Scott experienced a tragedy beyond comprehension. How does a father pick up the pieces and go on with life? My own experience in dealing with heartbroken parents tells me that they each have to deal with a painful loss in a personal manner. In Mr. Scott's case, he has become a dad on a mission. His mission is to write and speak about reaching out to others in compassion. In honoring his slain daughter, he hopes to develop a chain reaction for good over evil. His vision and subsequent cause is admirable and worthy of our attention in a book on leadership and service. Here are some of his thoughts I find particularly compelling.

> How do you begin to develop a lifestyle of reaching out and lending a helping hand? Here are three practical steps to get you started.[7]

1. Keep your eyes (and your heart) open
2. Slowdown
3. Make it a priority

In recounting a report of his daughter's last moments on earth, Scott relates a vivid, heartwenching scene as described by another student who was present. After firing three shots into Rachel

Scott's body,

> ...one of the killers reportedly grabbed Rachel by her hair, held her head up and asked her, "Do you believe in God?" "You know I do," replied Rachel. "Then go be with Him," he responded before shooting her in the head.[8]

From this awful scene, Scott moves on to remember his daughter as a student leader.

> At school she showed leadership not only by reaching out to other students but by giving her all to reach her goals in situations like the class play. Rachel had a servant's heart, but she wanted very desperately to star in the play, and she went after it. ...You are probably in a number of situations right now in which, if you decide to go for it and really work hard, you could grow into positions of leadership that are right for you. Take a look at your life and think of areas where you could make a contribution.[9]

At the university where I am employed, eighteen students died over the course of a six year span between 1994 and 2000. Most of the deaths resulted from automobile accidents. In dealing with devastated parents as well as a grieving campus, I have learned that death takes its toll on all of us, especially when the loss involves young promising lives. We are never prepared for it, simply because it is not supposed to happen that way. We tell ourselves the young should live. They should have their best years ahead of them. Of course, it is not for us to say. But when a young life is taken, I think of all that life had to offer. I then think of those who are left behind, people like Darrell Scott who has much to say in challenging others to lead and serve.

## DREAMS AS A SOURCE OF VISION

The Bible is full of examples of persons who became visionaries as a result of their dreams. I would certainly not discount the possibility of this happening in modern day lives. The topic of dreams, however, is rather deep for someone like myself. (My dreams are sometimes so bizarre that I am surely among the least qualified to write about them.) Let it suffice to point out that vision may be derived from an idea, an ideal, a conviction, a personal circumstance, or a dream.

Now that we have looked at the genesis of vision, let us consider the noble vision in relation to the workable vision. We will conclude by addressing the natural tension that exists between the two.

## THE NOBLE VISION

The Attorney General of the United States, John Ashcroft, has said "When you pursue noble things, sometimes noble things pursue you."[10] Those words were written well before the highly unusual events surrounding the 2000 election. The subsequent circumstances relating to Ashcroft—both during and in the immediate aftermath of his re-election campaign—seem to underscore the reality of his words.

After serving the state of Missouri for two full terms as Attorney General, two full terms as

Governor, and one term as a United States Senator, Ashcroft found himself in an almost unbelievable situation. Near the end of his bid for re-election to the Senate, Ashcroft's opponent, Governor Mel Carnahan, was killed in a tragic plane crash. After Lieutenant Governor Roger Wilson became Governor, he announced that he would appoint Carnahan's wife to the Senate seat of her late husband, should more votes be cast for Governor Carnahan than for Senator Ashcroft. In a narrow outcome charged with emotion and suspected voting irregularities (in locales favorable to the late Governor), Carnahan was declared the winner.

In remarks made to his staff during the early morning hours following election night, Ashcroft candidly addressed the situation in a personal way. "Like all of you, I am of course very sorry about tonight's outcome—more for all of you and the work you have done, than for me." The Senator went on to say "I don't know exactly why things worked out this way. I am certain, though, that God has a plan for all of us and that this is a part of it. I am having a very hard time right now trying to figure out what that purpose is, but I am certain He has one. I have great faith that somehow this is part of God's plan. If we only believe in God's plan and His will when it matches our own, that isn't faith. It is just observable knowledge. True faith is being confident in God when all of our own plans do not work out."

After a gracious concession, Ashcroft began to ponder his future. Then, the week before Christmas, he was nominated by President-Elect Bush to serve as Attorney General.

Even under normal circumstances, serving as the chief law enforcement officer of the United States would translate into an awesome responsibility. Add the major role Ashcroft has filled with respect to the war on terrorism, and the story becomes all the more remarkable.

Within a short period of time, John Ashcroft had made the transition from United States Senator to a high profile member of the President's cabinet. As one who has devoted his life to pursuing "noble things," Ashcroft found that a "noble thing" had once again pursued him.

Pursuing a noble vision is not just for persons in high places. For example, the vision may be related to spiritual revival. (Consider all that has been accomplished through the vision of Billy Graham.) The noble vision may point toward serving as an advocate for children or senior adults. Maybe it is to become pro-active in helping to curtail school violence or drug and alcohol use among young people. The list can go on and on. The important thing to remember is that once people have bought into the leader, they look to the leader to take them to higher ground. That is what the noble vision is all about in business, education, politics, and other walks of life.

## THE WORKABLE VISION

In essence, the workable vision may be defined as a virtuous goal that is transformed into a viable objective. Chapter Four describes how this may be accomplished.

## THE NOBLE VISION VS THE WORKABLE VISION

It is important to realize that a built-in tension exists between noble aspirations that tend to be idealistic in nature, and practical applications that demand realism. The leader can avoid a great deal of frustration by coming to grips with this fact as soon as possible.

The aforementioned tension is nothing new. The following example concerns Benjamin Franklin and his involvement in the American Revolution.

> Franklin was a practical man. Practical men usually do not make revolutions; dreamers do. Yet Benjamin Franklin became a revolutionary with several million others in America. His actions suggest one of the ironies of the American Revolution: its sources in a culture of men devoted to the hard realities of life—practical men, down-to-earth men like Franklin himself, men who in 1776 threw off their allegiance to the empire in the name of "common sense," a phrase that Thomas Pain had chosen as the title of his great tract on behalf of American independence.[11] (Used with permission from Oxford University Press. *The Glorious Cause - The American Revolution 1763-1789* by Robert Middlekauff.)

Earlier in this chapter a reference was made to Robert Kennedy and his passion for ideals. But notwithstanding those idealistic tendencies, Kennedy understood the need for pragmatism. The following account took place during the last months of his life. After having served as Attorney General of the United States, Kennedy had subsequently been elected as a United States Senator from the state of New York. This narrative by Dr. Robert Coles demonstrates how the noble vision may be spliced with the workable vision in order to better the lives of others.

> How to exert a certain kind of leadership—moral leadership—and be effective, get something good done: this was the lesson a group of us doctors learned in 1967 from encounters with Robert Kennedy—a lesson about how a moral purpose gets applied to the world in a practical way.
>
> We were a group of physicians who had spent time in the Mississippi Delta doing medical examinations of children. We were surprised at what we'd found—that in the United States there were still children suffering from malnutrition, vitamin deficiencies, and the diseases associated with them: beriberi, scurvy, rickets. We were more than surprised; at times we were stunned....
>
> In the late spring of 1967 we wrote up a substantial documentation of our observations... We were put in contact with high government officials... We wanted to spur them to action. Soon enough we were walking those long bureaucratic hallways in Washington, those corridors of American power."[12]

What the doctors found in those "corridors of American power," was discouragement. They could not seem to connect regarding their sense of urgency about a serious matter.

> We had talked with big shots, and they uniformly had given us the back of their hands... We were packing our bags when a phone message asked us to be in touch with Senator Robert Kennedy's Office... When we met Senator Kennedy he wasted no time with pleasantries. He had read what we had written, he told us; he had heard of our efforts to inform various government officials of our impressions and, too, of our collective sense that we'd been dismissed out of hand, even chastised.[13]

At this point, Coles and the other physicians were able to observe first hand how a noble vision can become a workable vision. The narrative continues:

> I believe Kennedy saw that our moral leadership was foundering on frustration—the unfortunate mix in us of high ideals not backed up by an understanding of how to get things done in the politics of the world.
>
> Days later we all met for lunch with Robert Kennedy and his aide, Peter Edelman, and one by one we spoke. The Senator listened with unremitting attentiveness—he was listening in order to act.
>
> Later we would all remark upon the sense we had that he was both glued to our

> words but constantly trying to estimate how others would react to them...[14]

In a follow-up meeting, Coles came face-to-face with the clash of noble vision vs workable vision. Much to his dismay, he found himself confronted by Kennedy's pragmatic instincts.

> I found those minutes troubling; they made me anxious and showed me the pragmatic, politically astute side of him... Yet in truth he was being protective of us by warning us of reality, of what to expect: he was bringing us down from our highfalutin innocence and idealistic moral high ground. He had, from the start, spotted a certain smugness in a few of us, a conviction on our part that we knew exactly what we were talking about and that accordingly we ought to be heeded, the sooner the better.[15]

After establishing a sense of realism, Kennedy was ready to move ahead. Before the physician's concerns would be brought before Congress, however, the doctors would accompany the Senator to some of the actual sites of their study.

> Soon enough, he was on the road and a bunch of us were in tow, watching and listening, sometimes pointing something out, more often attending what he had noticed and felt to be important. He had a way of holding himself back, a cool, reserved, calculating side, ever taking the measure of people, places, things, ever estimating costs and benefits; he also had a tentative,

> tender side, suddenly apparent, open and artless, fun-loving and mischievous—and that part of him connected quietly, almost wondrously with children... He visited the humble people of humble counties in Mississippi, in West Virginia; to see him sitting on the floor with the young, or bending over, or on his knees as they showed him something—shyly whispering their words of greeting to him, their answers to his queries, their declarations of desire or worry—was to see great influence and privilege also humbled.[16]
>
> After returning to Washington, Kennedy was serious about getting something done.
>
> ...He kept hearing in the Senate about leadership; all the time the word was spoken, as he put it, "leadership this and leadership that." ...This was serious business, he kept remarking in what for him was a monologue of sorts—"how to exert a certain kind of leadership." Then a second's hesitation, before the added qualification, "moral leadership," and then the final all important phrase, "and be effective."[17]

The previous narrative provides us with a vivid account of the noble vision and the workable vision coming together for the good of others. One without the other is a recipe for failure. A leader who is able to combine idealism with practicality is, I think, one who can make a difference in life.

## ITEMS FOR DISCUSSION

1. Explain the rationale for Maxwell's "Law of Buy In."
2. Identify and discuss five origins of vision.
3. Discuss the contrasting aspects of the noble vision vs the workable vision.
4. Identify an example of a noble vision.
5. Define workable vision.

## ENDNOTES

1. John C. Maxwell, *The 21 Irrefutable Laws of Leadership—Follow Them and People Will Follow You* (Nashville, Thomas Nelson, Inc., 1998), 145-146.

2. Florence Scovel Shinn, *The Game of Life & How to Play It* (New York: Fireside, 2001), 8-9. Reprinted with the permission of Simon & Schuster Adult Publishing Group. Copyright © 1925 by Florence Scovel Shinn.

3. Bill O'Reilly, *The O'Reilly Factor—The Good, The Bad, and The Completely Ridiculous in American Life* (New York: Broadway Books, 2000), 206.

4. Robert R. Kennedy, *To Seek A Newer World* (New York: Doubleday and Company, Inc., 1967), 233.

5. *Public Papers of The Presidents: John F. Kennedy*, (Washington, D.C.: 1962), 404.

6. John C. Maxwell, *The 21 Irrefutable Laws of Leadership—Follow Them and People Will Follow You*, 145-146.

7. Darrell Scott with Steve Rabey, *Chain Reaction—A Call To Compassionate Revolution* (Nashville: Thomas Nelson, Inc., 2001), 114-115.

8. Darrell Scott with Steve Rabey, *Chain Reaction—A Call To*

*Compassionate Revolution*, 126.

9. Darrell Scott with Steve Rabey, *Chain Reaction—A Call To Compassionate Revolution,* 128-129.

10. John Ashcroft with Gary Thomas, *Lessons From a Father to His Son* (Nashville: Thomas Nelson Publishers, 1998), 18.

11. Robert Middlekauff, *The Glorious Cause—The American Revolution 1763-1789* (New York: Oxford University Press, 1982), 3.

12. Robert Coles, *Lives of Moral Leadership* (New York: Random House. Copyright © 2000 by Robert Coles. Used by permission of Random House, Inc., 3-4.

13. Robert Coles, *Lives of Moral Leadership*, 5.

14. Robert Coles, *Lives of Moral Leadership*, 8.

15. Robert Coles, *Lives of Moral Leadership*, 15.

16. Robert Coles, *Lives of Moral Leadership*, 34.

17. Robert Coles, *Lives of Moral Leadership*, 37.

# Chapter Four:

# IMPLEMENTING THE VISION

**"Action springs not from thought, but from a readiness for responsibility."**
**Dietrich Bonhoeffer**

Having a vision without taking action to implement that vision is somewhat like owning a new car and never moving it out of the garage. This chapter, therefore, explores the necessary steps for carrying out one's vision. As illustrated below, implementing the vision involves a three step process.

| Step One: Enlisting Others | Step Two: Motivating Others | Step Three: Overseeing Others |
|---|---|---|

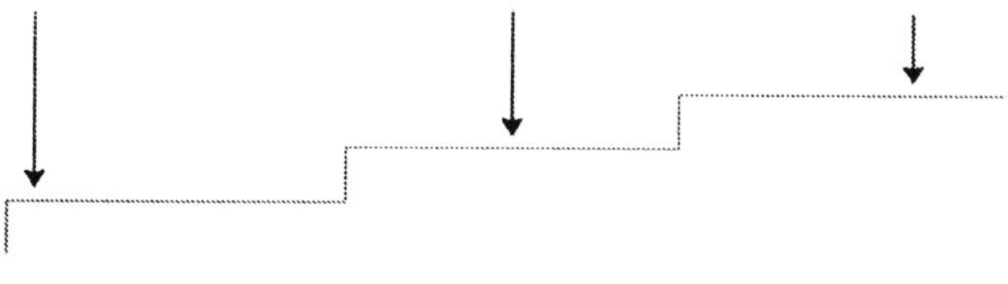

## ENLISTING OTHERS

A visionary will be quick to understand the importance of involving others in implementing his or her vision. The process of enlisting others may be guided by this self-imposed question: What characteristics am I looking for in the people I am striving to enlist?

The following list is not exhaustive. However, my experience has taught me that these personal traits are invaluable when it comes to implementing the vision.

1. Philosophical Compatibility
2. Commitment
3. Loyalty
4. Trustworthiness
5. Competence
6. Mature Judgement
7. Intelligence
8. Self-starter

### Philosophical Compatibility

Shortly after Bill Clinton was elected President of the United States in 1992, he made it known that he planned to enlist a cabinet that would mirror "the face of America." His intentions sounded like a good idea on the surface.

With due respect, however, I believe the fallacy of that standard is that it places the proverbial cart before the horse. It would seem that demographics should be secondary to finding the best individuals for the various posts. If the right people then collectively coincide with a diverse cross section, all the better.

One significant factor in choosing the right person for a particular assignment or position is philosophical compatibility. Why, you may ask, is it of utmost importance that everyone on your team share your philosophy? One answer is this: The leader is typically confronted by enough obstacles as it is. One impediment he or she can do without, is having a member of the group pulling in a different direction when the time comes to move ahead in implementing the vision.

This does not mean that the leader should be exempt from occasional dissent within the ranks. It is crucial, however, that the leader not be undermined once the decision is made to go forward.

When I made the transition from faculty to administration I found that I had walked into a prevailing tense atmosphere, one that appeared to engulf the Office of Student Life. It was evident to me that the office had come to reflect something of a "gotcha" mentality.

I immediately set out to change the climate in the office. I wanted students to view us as advocates rather than adversaries. Slowly but surely, over the course of a few years, the "us against them" reputation began to fade.

Thanks in large part to a dedicated staff (all of whom share my philosophy), the office has become a grand central station of sorts for undergraduates. To be sure, we still have to deal with serious problems when they arise. But even in that regard, I trust that most of our students do not believe that we are somehow out to get them.

### Commitment

A second trait to look for in enlisting others is commitment. One cannot overstate the significance of this vital characteristic. Simply put, commitment (or the lack thereof) has the potential to make or break the implementation of the vision.

When I am considering someone for a position, I try to discern a level of commitment on his or her part. For example, is the candidate primarily interested in what the job can do for him or her, or is he or she able to project a high level of commitment toward the job and all that it entails? Speaking for myself, I find it rather natural to take care of people's personal concerns once they have committed to the vision.

### Loyalty

In working to implement the vision, loyalty is a two way street. It is, I believe, unconscionable to expect loyalty unless one is prepared to give it.

Substantively speaking, loyalty is comprised of two facets. The first involves personal allegiance, a fact that is consistent with Maxwell's "Law of Buy In." The second aspect pertains to the vision and its implementation.

Personal loyalty requires a stalwart belief in the individual behind the vision. It is unavailing, I think, to count on someone to help realize the vision if that person's loyalty to the visionary is either uncertain or absent.

The leader can expect others to remain loyal to the vision if the vision is both noble and workable as discussed in Chapter Three. Once the follower locks in to the vision, he or she is generally in it for the long haul.

### Trustworthiness

Personal trust is a natural extension of personal loyalty. Thus, followers who are loyal to the visionary can generally be trusted to help expedite the vision. However, a word of caution is in order. Once lost, trust is very difficult to recover. The important thing to remember about trust – in the context of carrying out the vision – is that it should not be taken lightly, lest it be squandered.

### Competence

There are few things more frustrating for the leader than incompetent troops. That is particularly the case regarding the leader who tends to rely on delegation. The following check list may be beneficial in considering competent people to help carry out the vision.

Using the following scale, enter a self-evaluated numerical score in the blank space to the left of each competency.

Scale: 4 = above average, 3 = adequate,
2 = below average, and 1 = unsatisfactory

1. ___ Interactions with supervisor (Includes

the ability to follow instructions and complete assignments)

2. ___ Interactions with peers (Includes teamwork and the ability to cooperate)
3. ___ Interactions with subordinates (Includes supervisory skills)
4. ___ Public speaking skills
5. ___ Writing skills
6. ___ Organizational skills
7. ___ Technological skills
8. ___ Social skills (Includes the ability to get along with people in general)
9. ___ Personal Initiative skills
10. ___ Discerning skills (Includes the ability to be sensitive, insightful, and judicious)

Total _____

Key:
36 - 40 = above average
28 - 35 = adequate
20 - 27 = below average
10 - 19 = unsatisfactory

**Mature Judgement**

One of my all-time favorite television programs is The Andy Griffith Show (the black and white version). I am no doubt in good company when I point out that my favorite character is Barney Fife (as played by Don Knotts).

In episode after episode Barney displays a kind of judgement that falls short of the word "mature." More often than not, Barney is right on principle and wrong in his approach to the situation. In the end, Andy is always there to straighten things out.

The leader needs followers who are right on principle and approach. Both require mature judgement, and mature judgement comes down to making the right call, at the right time, for the right reason.

### Intelligence

Another quality the leader should seek out on the part of his or her followers is intelligence. When enlisting others to help implement the vision, the leader would do well to remember that smart people are apt to do smart things.

### Self-Starter

The final trait on this list is the ability to function as a self-starter. This does not mean that the follower should be free to operate independently. Instead, the leader should make effective use of the self-starter by establishing clear parameters, keeping the lines of communication open, and maximizing his or her strengths.

An effective leader will make a conscious effort to grow other leaders. Thus, when implementing the vision, the leader should keep in mind that a self-starter is a leader in the making.

## MOTIVATING OTHERS

The second step in implementing the vision is that of motivating others to act. This step also has some application for enlisting the services of others (step one), and involves at least four underlying practices. They are:

1. Finding common ground
2. Communicating purpose and direction
3. Empowerment
4. Acknowledgement

**Finding Common Ground**

The leader must be able to recognize the fundamental nature of discovering a common link with his or her followers. Without this motivating connection, other attempts at motivating will prove less effective.

James M. Kouzes and Barry Z. Posner have much to say about the importance of common ground. They point out the need to:

> Enlist others in a common vision by appealing to their Values, Interests, Hopes, and Dreams... ...In order to attract people from diverse backgrounds and interests, you must discover what aspirations, goals, needs, and dreams they have in common. They're bound to differ in much of what they value; you must work through the differences to find what can bring them together... ...To have the broadest appeal, visions must be encompassing. They should transcend the day-to-day work (voluntary or paid) and find expression in higher-order human needs. Visions should uplift and enable.[1]

The motivational affect of addressing shared needs cannot be overstated. Here are some additional insights and suggestions.

(1.) Discover and address the most urgent needs of others. When a sense of urgency exists, so too does an opportunity for finding common ground.

(2.) Envision how your vision and another person's need can be intertwined for the purpose of fulfilling both. While some may contend that this smacks of manipulation, I tend to side with the view expressed by Alan Loy McGinnis with respect to bringing out the best in people.

> You are a manipulator when you try to persuade people to do something that is not in their best interests but is in yours. You are a motivator when you find goals that will be good for both sides, then weld together a high-achieving, high-morale partnership to achieve them.[2]

(3.) Strive to provide a realistic sense of hope for a positive outcome. There are obviously two key words in this challenge. One is "*realistic.*" (Pipe dreams can do more harm than good.) A second key term is "*hope.*" As discussed in Chapter Two, followers look to the leader for a sense of hope.

(4.) Look for ways to act as a facilitator, rather than an inhibitor. This fits well with the old saying "where there is a will, there is a way."

(5.) Strive to develop a shared sense of destiny

as well as shared goals and objectives. Have you ever noticed how when two people take a long "road trip" together they often arrive at their destination with a fuller appreciation for each other? That is the idea behind sharing a sense of destiny rather than just a sense of purpose.

(6.) Maintain a personal tie between leader and follower. The act of finding common ground with others demands personalization if it is to be effective. One of my favorite stories in that regard is told by David Herbert Donald in his outstanding biography on the life of Abraham Lincoln. In describing the long train ride from Springfield, Illinois to Washington, D.C. – where Lincoln was to be inaugurated as the sixteenth President of the United States – Donald tells of the President-Elect's encounters with American citizens along the way.

> The stated object of this round about journey was to give the people an opportunity to become acquainted with their new Chief Executive, the first American President to be born west of the Appalachian Mountains. To satisfy this natural curiosity Lincoln made very frequent appearances at the rear of the train, where, as he said, he could offer people the opportunity "of observing my

> very interesting countenance." Presently he developed a formula that he used repeatedly: he came before the public, he announced, so "that I may see you and you may see me, and in the arrangement I have the best of the bargain." He could afford to joke because he generally made a favorable impression.[3]

I like this little reference because it is both simple and powerful. Long before the days of television news, Lincoln learned how to connect with the public in a personal way. My hunch is that by the time the train pulled into Washington's Union Station, Honest Abe had found common ground with thousands who may or may not have actually voted for him.

(7.) Finally, in maintaining that all-important common ground, the leader must be able to perpetuate his or her personal credibility. (See Chapter Eight.)

**Communicating Purpose and Direction**

In addition to finding common ground, the leader should be prepared to motivate others by communicating purpose and direction. In so doing, the leader will avoid confusion and doubt.

Purpose is essential. In motivating people to stay the course, it will be necessary to keep purpose in the forefront of all that is said and done. That is why succient mission statements have become so prevalent among various organizations.

Communicating direction is also vital. A good leader will know where things are headed, even when adjustments are necessary. Followers tend to be motivated by someone who is able to point the way to an appealing new horizon.

### Empowerment

Empowerment is more than simply involving others. Empowerment motivates others by giving them a sense of ownership. It is one thing to talk about teamwork. It is something else for each member of the team to feel that he or she is an integral part of its reason for existence.

As a motivational technique, empowerment can be useful to the leader in several respects. Rick Lynch and Sue Vineyard point out "five dimensions of empowerment that leaders recognize."[4]

> (1.) SIGNIFICANCE:
> Helping others to feel legitimately important and that they are truly making a difference by their efforts. The leader helps people understand where they are all going and how each part is critical to the end result, no matter how "small"their part seems to be... The leader constantly reminds all involved of the overall significance the organization is making in the lives of others, by keeping the mission at the forefront of thinking. In so doing, the leader keeps the

focus on PEOPLE not THINGS...

(2.) COMPETENCE:

Enabling people to learn and develop on the job; increasing their sense of mastery. Leaders see work places as settings for continual learning. They support this through coaching, teaching, training and the encouragement (both verbally and tangibly) of continuing education opportunities related to the work to be done. Leaders reward creativity, innovation, problem solving and new ideas for maximum efficiency and effectiveness... Leaders are not threatened by "better ideas" or the competence of their people, even when it falls in an area considered to be the expertise of the leader...they take great pride and joy in empowering such people to stretch to the limits of their competence and beyond, so that their joint contributions can enhance the vision of the group.

(3.) COMMUNITY:

Leaders understand the importance of everyone feeling joined in a common purpose and keep this purpose or vision before everyone's eyes. They establish a climate of trust and risk-taking, encouraging anyone to question anything if they feel they have a better perspective or way of doing things... They empower people to create community-building activities, encouraging them to plan and execute them as they see fit. They reward such activities openly. They participate fully in efforts that build relationships among workers and influence those efforts so that a focus is kept on the joint purpose and shared vision of the group.

(4.) ENJOYMENT:
Leaders empower people by modeling their value of a sense of adventure and play. They create a climate that encourages fun, warmth, and sense of pleasure. They catch people being good and reward them for it. They foster creativity and enjoyment that benefits everyone (even those that have buried the child in them and cannot openly "play" or have fun.) They do not force playfulness on everyone, but they clearly give "permission" for some voluntarily... They bring out the child in people, understanding that this characteristic can reduce tension, stress and strain while causing bubbles of creative thinking to rise to the surface...

(5.) POWER:
Leaders define work so that people have something to be in charge of . Rather than merely assigning tasks, they give people meaningful responsibility for results. In doing so, the leader gives people a sense of having something to control. They thus provide a challenge and a sense of purpose.

I would be remiss at this point if I failed to stress that there are various levels of empowerment. While empowering others on an evenhanded basis may seem proper, reality dictates otherwise.

It is therefore not unusual for the leader to reserve a special niche for the few who make up his or her inner circle. The inner circle consists of the leader's most trusted confidants. Although experience, ability, and similar attributes are important, they are not necessarily predominate among those who are included in this category. Instead, the essential qualities are trust, confidence, and chemistry.

The inner circle is typically small in number. Some tend to be more discriminating than others in their inclusions. In my own case, I admit to being very selective. For example, I got to know Courtney Stalker when she was a college student. She has since become a member of my staff. Because we tend to think in a similar manner, and as a result of an established high level of trust, I find myself turning to her often as a member of this exclusive group.

Two visual illustrations help depict how the inner circle idea works. (See "Understanding the Inner Circle" and "Organizational Chart vs Inner Circle Concept.")

### Acknowledgment

It is both appropriate and wise to acknowledge the contributions of others. Acknowledgment may take the form of a personal word of gratitude spoken in private, or some type of public recognition. In either case, the leader will find that acknowledging the input of others is an effective motivational tool.

Rick Lynch and Sue Vineyard cite the following "Rules For Recognition"[5]

## UNDERSTANDING THE INNER CIRCLE

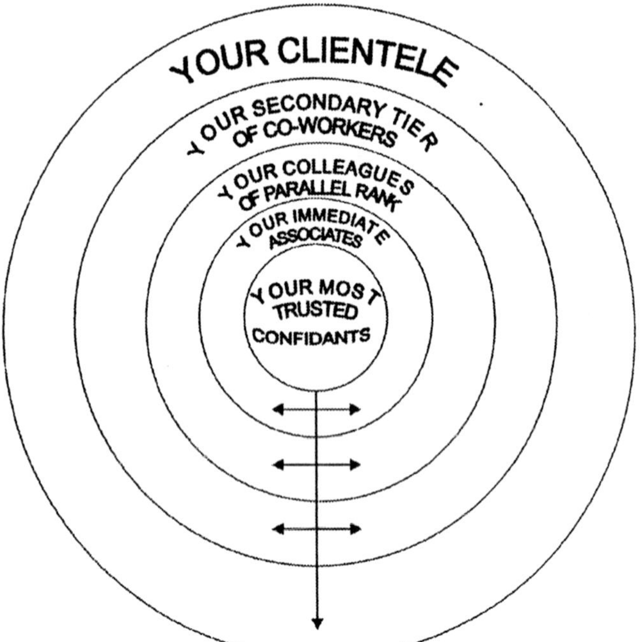

**<u>ORGANIZATIONAL CHART</u> vs. <u>INNER CIRCLE CONCEPT</u>**

**Emphasis On:**

| | | |
|---|---|---|
| 1. Management Process | ↔ | 1. Leadership Manner |
| 2. Work Flow | ↔ | 2. Personal Chemistry |
| 3. Lines of authority for all | ↔ | 3. Exclusive "membership" for a few confidants |
| 4. Work environment designed to accomplish immediate responsibilities | ↔ | 4. Climate of trust that bridges the present and future |

(1.) *Give it frequently.* In a three year survey of workers in non-profit and government organizations, Lynch Associates found that over seventy-five percent felt they did not get enough recognition. The reason for this feeling is that recognition has a short shelf life. This week's smile, pat on the back, note, or certificate does not guarantee that the person will still feel you value him and his efforts next month.

(2.) *It must be varied.* If we are to give it often, we need to use a variety of ways to recognize others... Be creative! Have fun! Find new ways to say "Thank You."

(3.) *It must be honest.* As indicated earlier, credibility is an extremely important trait in a leader. If you praise people not because you mean it but because you think it might persuade them to do better work, they (and everyone else you supervise) will detect it. It will cheapen the recognition everyone else gets and force the person who received the insincere expression to either conclude that you don't know the difference between mediocre and good work or that you are a manipulative and untrustworthy person.

(4.) *It should be given to the person,* not to the work. This is a subtle point but an important one. If the work is praised without mentioning the person who did it, the person will feel resentment. Similarly, if the group as a whole is given credit for what a few people did, the few who did the work will resent it. Say "You did a great job on this," not "This is good work."

(5.) *It should be appropriate to the achievement...* Small deeds should receive recognition that require little effort and big deeds should get recognized in ways that take more time and money.

(6.) *It should be consistent.* If one person receives recognition for an action, another person who does something similar should receive a similar reward. Otherwise, people start to feel you are playing favorites.

(7.) *It must be timely.* If recognition is not given until much after the event, the person will feel unappreciated in the meantime.

(8.) *It should be individualized* as much as possible. Different people respond to different means of recognition. One person might respond well to a hug, while another might recoil at the idea of being touched and another might even sue you for sexual harassment! Leaders get to know their people so they can show appreciation in a manner valued by the other. Remember: recognition is user-oriented.

(9.) *Reward what you want more of.* This may seem rather obvious, but it is not the natural instinct of most people, particularly in the human service field. Instead, the natural tendency is to focus our attention on the people who are not performing acceptable, trying to find out what's wrong, offering counseling, coaching, and nurturing. Although these are important management activities, the danger is that the good performers wind up feeling ignored and unappreciated. Sometimes, capable workers even begin to manufacture problems, just to get some attention from the leader. Leaders focus on what is going *right* and praise it. In order to get praise and attention, marginal performers may start to do better.

(10.) *Give it or else.* This last rule is a warning. Recognition is one of the most powerful of all human motivators. If people do not get recognition from the leader for good work they may seek other places to work or volunteer. Or worse, they may start to get recognition from their peers for counterproductive behavior.

## OVERSEEING OTHERS

The final step in implementing the vision is a natural continuation of the first two steps (enlisting others and motivating others). In overseeing those who are helping to achieve the vision, the leader will monitor progress while keeping things on course. These primary verities will be useful in that regard:

(1.) Keep in mind that goals and objectives should trump policies, programs, and initiatives. It is sometimes difficult to maintain a focus when details become the order of the day. It is the leader's responsibility to keep purpose in the forefront. A good leader will recognize that policies, programs, and initiatives should serve as means to ends rather than ends in themselves.

(2.) In overseeing others, the leader should employ a leadership style that works for him or her. I have purposefully refrained from discussing the classic leadership styles due to a belief that they are, in reality, management styles. Still, the leader will find that he or she leans toward one of two methods.

The first is a "hands on" approach. Some leaders feel the need to maintain as much control as possible in directing others. Thus, they tend to be involved in the details of working toward the achievement of the vision. My advice for those who are inclined to make use of this approach is twofold. First, beware of getting too bogged down in the details. Second, realize that effective subordinates respond best to leaders who avoid being overly intrusive.

That brings us to the second approach which is to rely more on delegation and broad direction. Effective followers tend to flourish under this method. A word of advice for leaders who employ this type of modus operandi: keep the lines of communication open!

As observed in this chapter, implementing the vision is a matter of enlisting others, motivating others, and overseeing others. When done properly, these three procedures can help transform a vision into a reality.

## ITEMS FOR DISCUSSION

1. Explain the importance of philosophical compatibility in enlisting others to help implement the vision.
2. In motivating others to act, explain why finding common ground is important.
3. Identify and explain the level of empowerment for which the leader will reserve a special niche.
4. Discuss the role of acknowledgment as a motivational tool.
5. Identify and explain two verities that are useful in overseeing others.

## ENDNOTES

1. James M. Kouzes and Barry Z. Posner, *The Leadership Challenge* (San Francisco: Jossey-Bass, 1995), 141. Reprinted by permission of John Wiley & Sons, Inc.

2. Alan Loy McGinnis, *Bringing Out The Best In People – How to Enjoy Helping Others To Excel* (Minneapolis: Augsburg Publishing House, 1985), 21.

3. Reprinted with the permission of Simon & Schuster from *Lincoln* by David Herbert Donald. Copyright © 1995 by David Herbert Donald, 274.

4. Rick Lynch and Sue Vineyard, *Secrets of Leadership* (Downers Grove, Illinois: Heritage Arts Publishing, 1991), 37-38.

5. Rick Lynch and Sue Vineyard, *Secrets of Leadership,* 33-34.

# PART TWO: SERVICE

## Chapter Five:

# SELFLESSNESS AND SERVICE

**"The secret of being loved
is in being lovely;
and the secret in being lovely
is in being unselfish."
Josiah Gilbert Holland**

A case can be made that selflessness is to service, what influence is to leadership. As a key part of service, the act of selflessness may be broken down into four segments. These include:

1. Self-denial (yielding)
2. Self-sacrifice (love)
3. Self-discipline (integrity)
4. Self-deprecation (humility)

### SELF-DENIAL

The Christian belief regarding the practice of self-denial is inherent in the act of service. Perhaps that is why many perceive service as a natural extension of faith. In the words of Aiden Wilson Tozer, "When you empty yourself, God Almighty rushes in."[1]

By its nature, service to others is something that takes place apart from our more instinctive egocentric desires. Thus, to serve well, one must be capable of employing a measure of self-denial. The greater the degree of self-denial, the more meaningful will be the act of service.

There is, perhaps, no greater contemporary rendering of self-denial than the heroic examples associated with the September 11, 2001 terrorists attacks on America. The following words of President George W. Bush describe the kind of self-denial required of those who defend freedom:

> A commander-in-chief sends America's sons and daughters into a battle in a foreign land only after the greatest care and a lot of prayer. We ask a lot of those who wear our uniform. We ask them to leave their loved ones, to travel great distances, to risk injury, even to be prepared to make the ultimate sacrifices of their lives...[2]

## SELF-SACRIFICE

Tragically, many paid the ultimate price on September 11, 2001. While most of us will not be called on to pay that same price, we will nonetheless have opportunities to sacrifice for the sake of others.

Leslie Lenkowsky oversees many who regularly engage in the practice of self-sacrifice. Appointed by

President Bush to serve as the Chief Executive Officer for the Corporation for National and Community Service, Lenkowsky was kind enough to meet with me in April of 2002. We met in his Washington, D.C. office to discuss sacrificial service in the post-September 11, 2001 climate of America. Following are excerpts from that interview.

> **Question:** Explain the organizational structure for the President's new emphasis on service in America.
>
> **Answer:** U.S.A. Freedom Corps is the umbrella for the overall effort. John Bridgeland is the Executive Director.
>
> Think of Freedom Corps as an organizational parallel to the National Security Council, and Bridgeland as an organizational counterpart to (National Security Adviser) Condoleezza Rice. Both report to the President. Freedom Corps is run by a Board of Directors which the President chairs.
>
> The Corporation for National and Community Service is within the umbrella of Freedom Corps, but operates as a legally independent arm.
>
> **Question:** What changes have you observed in the way of volunteer spirit in the aftermath of 9-11?
>
> **Answer:** There is a new spirit in the country for volunteering. So far, however, there is not a lot of evidence that activities have increased. Attitudes have changed, but

volunteers still have to be asked. To encourage involvement, the President has challenged Americans to complete 4,000 hours of service during their lifetimes.

**Question:** What else can be done to encourage involvement?

**Answer:** Private institutions need to reach out.

**Question:** What are some of the personal benefits of voluntary service?

**Answer:** Young people develop skills and knowledge for later use. Social development is also a benefit. I met my wife through involvement in service. Patriotism is another benefit. President Bush refers to it as a "culture of citizenship, service, and responsibility."

**Question:** Can you share a recent success story that demonstrates service and self-sacrifice?

**Answer:** We sent people to Kansas City when the ice storm occurred. We also sent people to Salt Lake City during the Olympics to serve as back-ups for local officials.

Then there is a story of Red Hook, New York, located in the lower part of New York City. Seven years ago, this impoverished area was designated for a project by AmeriCorps (which is part of the Corporation for National and Community Service). The project involved things like neighborhood clean-up and block-watch programs. On September 11, fire fighters from Red Hook were among the first to arrive at the site of the twin towers. Two dozen lost their lives. The residents of Red Hook and volunteers from AmeriCorps worked tirelessly to load beverages onto trucks for those who were doing all they could to save lives.

After completing the interview, I stood to make my way out of Lenkowsky's office. As he walked with me to the area immediately outside of his office, he added a final comment that bears repeating. He said, "volunteering may be free, but it's not easy." Those who sacrifice self for the good of others know the truth of that statement.

The Corporation for National and Community Service has three divisions:[3]

1. Learn and Serve America
2. AmeriCorps National Service
3. National Senior Service Corps

CORPORATION

FOR NATIONAL

AND

COMMUNITY

SERVICE

Throughout our nation, many schools
incorporate service-learning—
a teaching method
that connects classroom studies with
community service.

Learn and serve America volunteers plan their next community service project.

A Learn and Serve America volunteer gives an infant a piggy-back ride during playtime.

More than 50,000 AmeriCorps members serve our nation through intensive community service while earning money for education.

AmeriCorps members plan a community service project.

An AmeriCorps member organizes supplies at the Red Cross Family Services Center in New York City after the September 11 terrorist attack.

Nearly half a million Americans age 55 and older use their time and talents to help solve pressing community problems through one of three Senior Corps Programs:
Foster Grandparents
Senior Companions
and RSVP

A volunteer with the Senior Companion program assists another senior with paying his bills.

A Foster Grandparent reads a book to his foster "granddaughter"

In her senior essay on what it means to be a servant leader, Courtney Stalker discusses an idea related to self-sacrifice. It is a concept she learned while attending the National Student Leadership Forum held in Washington, D.C. "Another concept that was presented in D.C. was that we should strive to work beyond our ambitions. I have always heard that it is important to have a passion for what you do and truly love it, but I hadn't really thought of working beyond the goals that I have. I think that is partly because I do set high goals for myself and those I work with, but that is no excuse not to strive for more."

## SELF-DISCIPLINE

Working to achieve goals, and working beyond those goals, requires self-discipline. If self-sacrifice represents an act of love, self-discipline denotes the practice of integrity. In deliberating on the importance of self-discipline, several considerations should be kept in mind.

First, all leaders are an example for others. The question is what kind of an example does one wish to set? To set a positive example in service, one must be willing to engage in self-discipline.

Second, the leader who is intent on self-discipline should not hesitate to be his or her own worst critic. I am not suggesting that leaders should bash themselves when they make mistakes. Instead, they should realize that self-discipline necessitates introspective thinking and some degree of personal objectivity.

Third, the leader should establish and follow certain parameters. This is basically a matter of acting rather than reacting.

Fourth, the leader who serves others should strive to keep things in perspective. It is easy for one to be so close to a given situation, that one is unable to see the forest for the trees.

Fifth, the leader should guard against naivete'. The leader would do well to be open-minded rather than defensive when it comes to listening to those he or she finds most trustworthy.

Sixth, the leader should not serve unless he or she is able to be devoted to the cause. By being dedicated to something, one defines who he or she is.

Seventh, one who leads and serves must be sensitive regarding the issue of perceived conflicts of interest (whether or not an actual conflict of interest exists). It is a good idea to keep in mind that perception can be reality.

Finally, self-discipline requires both short term energy and long term resolve. The leader who serves others will therefore recognize the need for developing personal activities that aid his or her capacity for service.

## SELF-DEPRECATION

The final segment of selflessness in service is self-deprecation, or humility. The practice of self-deprecation must be accompanied by a sincere humble spirit. From there it extends to an outward display of genuine modesty.

Humility as demonstrated by self-deprecation is, I think, one of the secrets of effective leadership and service. In addition to keeping the leader from being "over the heads" of those he or she serves, self-deprecation can add humor and a down-to-earth atmosphere to a given situation.

Former Senator Bob Dole recognizes the importance of self-deprecation. Following is a sampling of examples that he has compiled.[4]

> **Abraham Lincoln:** After his perennial rival, Stephen A. Douglas, called him two-faced, Lincoln turned to his audience and drawled, "I leave it to you. If I had another face, do you think I would wear this one?"
>
> **John F. Kennedy:** Kennedy was not above parodying the soaring rhetoric of his own inaugural address. Before a fund-raising dinner of loyal Democrats, he announced sententiously: "We observe tonight, not a celebration of freedom but a victory of party, for we have sworn to pay off the same party debt our forebears ran up nearly a year and three months ago. Our deficit will not be paid off in the next one hundred days, nor will it be paid off in the first one thousand days, nor in the life of this administration. Nor, perhaps, even in our lifetime on this planet. But let us begin."
>
> Kennedy was just as ironic in describing his wartime experiences aboard PT109. Asked by a reporter how he became a war hero, the President replied, "It was absolutely involuntary. They sank my boat."

At a July 1963 press conference, JFK was reminded of his 1960 campaign pledge to get America moving again. "Do you think it is moving?" asked a reporter. "And if so, how and where? The reason I ask you the question, Mr. President, is that the Republican National Committee recently adopted a resolution saying you are pretty much a failure." "I'm sure it was passed unanimously," replied Kennedy.

**Lyndon Johnson:** Johnson liked to begin speeches with an unaccustomed touch of verbal humility. "I wish my mother and father might have been here to hear that introduction," he would observe. "My father would have enjoyed it, and my mother would have believed it."

**Ronald Reagan:** Reagan was a master at self-deprecation, especially on the subject of his age. "When I was in the fifth grade," he once said, "I'm not sure that I knew what a national debt was. Of course, when I was in the fifth grade, we didn't have one."

**George Bush (the first President Bush):** In one commencement speech former President Bush half-threatened to spend forty-five minutes talking about the Federal Reserve Board, followed by half an hour on the gold standard. He then relented, inspired by a story he attributed to the Reverend Billy Graham. It con-

> cerned a long-winded speaker whose oration droned on endlessly, until a man at the head table picked up his shoe, threw it at the speaker's podium, missed his target, and struck a lady in the front row instead. "Hit me again," she said, "I can still hear him."

As with other aspects of leadership and service, humility requires effort. Amber Slayton, an attorney living and serving in the Dallas-Fort Worth, Texas area, explains why the effort is worthwhile.

> "Two of the most difficult traits to maintain are humility and selflessness. So often, people who have a servant's heart assume a leadership position and become driven by power. Even students who are elected to positions on campus, such as class president, can fall victim to self-importance. A failure to maintain a sense of humility and selflessness will cause a person to stop listening to those he or she serves, and start working to feed his or her ego rather than attend to the constituents' needs. Numerous Greek tragedies were written about this weakness of man, and many historical and biblical figures fell victim to this."

Thus, as we have observed in this chapter, selflessness plays a vital part in service. May those who commit to serving the needs of others, be ready to fill that all important role.

## ITEMS FOR DISCUSSION

1. Discuss U.S.A. Freedom Corps and its national role in promoting voluntary service.
2. Discuss the personal benefits of voluntary service.
3. Discuss the following statement of Leslie Lenkowsky: "Volunteering may be free, but it is not easy."
4. Identify and explain important considerations in self-discipline.
5. Explain how humility, as demonstrated by self-deprecation, is a secret of effective leadership and service.

## ENDNOTES


1. Martin H. Manser, *The Westminster Collection of Christian Quotations* (Louisville: Westminster John Knox Press, 2001), 389.

2. David Hayes, "George W. Bush—The Making of a Wartime President" (Commemorative Issue), *American Media Specials Inc.* Vol. II No. 4 (2001): 57.

3. All pictures, captions, and logos from Compact Disc produced by Jacqueline Aker, Corporation for National and Community Service, Washington, D.C., used by permission.

4. Bob Dole, *Great Presidential Wit...I Wish I Was in This Book* (New York: Scribner, 2001), 14, 80, 81, 97, 47, 131.

# Chapter Six:

# THE PROCESS OF SERVING OTHERS

**"We make a living by what we get, but we make a life by what we give."**
**Sir Winston Churchill**

If selflessness in service is attitudinal–a reflection of that which we are, the serving process is characterized by action–something we do. To fully engage in the process of service, one should first be familiar with its essential ingredients and necessary steps.

At least four elements are intrinsic in the process of service to others. They are:

1. Empathy
2. Encouragement
3. Facilitation
4. Appreciation

## THE EMPATHY COMPONENT

Empathy may be viewed as a key that effectively unlocks the door to human service. Without genuine empathy, other ingredients in the process of service are superficial at best.

In displaying empathy, one simultaneously reveals a capacity for sensitivity regarding the needs of others. This is paramount in that empathy calls for one to place oneself in the circumstance of another individual. Fulfilling this requirement is not automatic–and in fact demands substantial effort–given our more natural instincts to primarily be concerned with our own sets of circumstances.

Perhaps the most consistent modern example of empathy may be found in the life of Agnes Bojaxhiu, the legendary Mother Teresa of Calcuta, India. Up until the time of her death in 1997, this physically small but spiritually strong woman seemed to embody the essence of empathy. Her words continue to resonate.

> Today it is fashionable to talk about the poor. Unfortunately, it is not fashionable to talk with them...
>
> A way of satisfying our brethren's hunger is to share with them whatever we have–to share with them until we ourselves feel what they feel.[1]

Few, of course, will emulate Mother Teresa's example. Still, empathy is not limited by environment and its principles are all-inclusive.

One of the more useful axioms I have come across is found in "the Principle of Empathetic

Communication," as brought forward by Stephen R. Covey.

> ...Seek First to Understand, Then to Be Understood... Perhaps the most powerful principle of all human interaction: genuinely seeking to understand another deeply before being understood in return. At the root of all interpersonal problems is failure to throughly understand each other. The actual disagreements of substance are magnified and compounded by our inability to see the world not only through another's eyes, but also through his or her mind and heart. We misunderstand and therefore mistrust motives, points of view–we are so ego-invested in advancing our own ideas, defending our position, attacking contrary opinion, judging, evaluating, probing, and questioning–that we normally listen with the intent not to understand but to respond... True empathetic communication shares faithfully not only words, ideas, and information, but also feelings, emotions, and sensitivities.[2]

Two former U.S. Presidents offer cases-in-point. When candidate Bill Clinton told jobless Americans in 1992 that he "felt their pain," a perception of empathy formed in the minds of many voters. As President, Clinton continued to be perceived as an empathetic leader. An earlier reference was made (in Chapter Two) to President Lyndon Johnson's take on power. But notwithstanding certain idiosyncrasies,

Johnson, it seems, was quite adept when it came to an ability to feel and express empathy.

> ...It may seem all the more surprising that a man with his towering ego should have climbed to such heights by studying the inner as well as the outer needs of others. Yet it was his willingness to focus on other people and their concerns, no matter how small, that contributed to the near total communication... Johnson achieved with those he sought to influence.
>
> Jack Brooks, a Texas congressman who had been a close friend of LBJ and knew the "Johnson Treatment" first hand, told me that it came down to an extraordinary ability to concentrate the entire mind on his target's immediate situation. "Lyndon Johnson would convince you that your concern, no matter how small it might seem to other people, was the most important thing in the world to Lyndon Johnson."[3]

## THE ENCOURAGEMENT COMPONENT

If empathy opens the door to service, encouragement enables one to stay inside. Furthermore, encouragement is an aspect of service that is difficult to measure, but nonetheless real. I like these words of George M. Adams: "Encouragement is oxygen to the soul."[4]

Nancy was a college freshman who came to my office one day in tears. It seems she had not been able to get her financial aid package settled. To make matters worse, she had just come from the office of her academic advisor who had gently tried to suggest that "maybe college is not for you." (Although she had to deal with a learning disability, Nancy was a determined student whose goal was to someday teach others with learning disabilities.)

Nancy informed me that her parents were in route to campus (a three hour drive). She had phoned them to say she was ready to drop out of school. While I knew we would eventually need to address her financial aid situation and seek to provide some type of academic assistance, I quickly realized that her most urgent need was for some good old fashioned encouragement. I did the best I could, and by the time her parents arrived she seemed to feel better.

To make a long story short, we put a plan in place that enabled her to stay in school. To her credit, Nancy is now a successful teacher. As a result of that experience, I have concluded that a little encouragement can go a long way.

Amanda was also in need of encouragement. As a college freshman, she had become a member of the spirit squad. After only one semester as a cheerleader, she was unable to continue her participation in this activity due to impending surgery.

In and out of hospitals over the next several years, Amanda found herself battling a painfully debilitating physical condition that threatened her ability to walk. Beyond her physical difficulties, she faced additional hurdles related to an increasing number of class absences. After leaving school for a brief time, Amanda returned to give it one more try. She acquired a local job. She enrolled in classes to pursue a degree in athletic training and psychology. Her physical condition slowly but surely improved. Before long, it was apparent that Amanda had turned the corner. Today, she will tell anyone who wants to listen how the encouragement of others sustained her through some tough times.

## THE FACILITATION COMPONENT

Edgar Z. Friedenberg has said "what we must decide is how we are valuable rather than how valuable we are."[5] These words provide a context for facilitation as part of the serving process.

Kelli was a second semester junior in college when she approached me one spring afternoon with the idea of starting a Habitat for Humanity chapter on campus. After I had explained the necessary steps for initiating a new campus organization, I encouraged her to investigate the external requirements for affiliating with this well-established international organization.

Within a week, Kelli excitedly reported her findings. We would soon be on our way toward the development of a campus chapter that would afford new service opportunities for many.

First, however, the new group would need an advisor. My initial inclination was to inform Kelli that she would have to locate a member of the faculty or staff who would be willing to serve in such a capacity. Then, I thought better of that approach.

Two factors led me to volunteer as the advisor

for the first year. First, I was concerned that Kelli might experience difficulty in finding someone who would readily agree to take on an extra responsibility. (I hoped to ward off any early discouragement on her part.) Second, I was uniquely well-positioned to help transform this idea into a reality. In short, it would be my privilege to serve as a facilitator.

As a result of Kelli's leadership and commitment, things began to fall into place. We soon learned that local townspeople were moving forward to establish a community chapter. Now it would be possible for college students and community residents to work side-by-side in a worthwhile endeavor. In May, we received word that the founder of Habitat for Humanity, Millard Fuller, had agreed to speak on our campus at the beginning of the fall semester. Then, over the summer, we were notified that we had been officially approved as a campus chapter. An idea for service had become a reality.

## THE APPRECIATION COMPONENT

In Chapter Four we considered acknowledgment and its rightful role in leadership. A related and more deep-seated notion is that of appreciation.

Acknowledgment represents a calculated act, while appreciation reflects a steadfast high regard. Thus, acknowledgment is actually a by-product of appreciation.

In serving, one should be <u>appreciative</u> of the immanent worth of others-be they fellow laborers or those on the receiving end of service. This type of appreciation manifests itself in the form of genuine respect.

The ideal of treating others as one would wish to be treated is, of course, all about respect. David Neidert testifies to its virtues.

> The Golden Rule makes revolutionary sense today as it has for the past two millennia. This relationship measurement makes sense simply because it takes you to the deepest recesses of how you want to be treated as a human being.
>
> ...Searching for the highest good in human nature reveals not only your desired treatment, but makes you sensitive to the treatment sought by others. ...In the end, the Golden Rule is the sum total of all the leadership books on this planet.[6]

Charles C. Manz points out that respect can pave the way for further respect, and disrespect can lead to disregard.

> Think for a moment about the ways you have been treated by various authority figures throughout your life. I suspect that you will recognize the simple fact that when you were treated disrespectfully, as an unworthy person of little value, not only did your view of yourself suffer but so did your view of the leader. The leaders for whom you were willing to go the extra mile were likely the ones that went an extra mile for you, the ones who believed in you even when you screwed up, the ones who recognized your great potential, your full

value as a unique person.[7]

John Wooden is another staunch believer in the importance of respect. The highly successful retired head mens basketball coach of the UCLA Bruins was known to have practiced what he continues to preach. According to Wooden, respect is a two-way street.

> The most essential thing for a leader to have is the respect of those under his or her supervision. It starts with giving them respect.
>
> You must make it clear that you are working together. Those under your supervision are not working for you but with you and you all have a common goal. ...If they don't respect their leader, people just punch the clock in and out. There is not clock-watching when a leader has respect...[8]

And how does one earn respect? Again, Coach Wooden weighs in with what he calls "The Value in Feeling Valued."

> Everyone on the team, from the manager to the coach, from a secretary to an owner, has a role to fulfill. That role is valuable if the team is to come close to reaching its potential. The leader must understand this.
>
> ...Right after each UCLA basketball game, there would be a press conference with representatives from all the media. I could predict what questions they would ask

> and which players they wanted to interview.
>
> I always tried to use this opportunity to praise those individuals the media would overlook. I would say "when I put so-and-so in just before the half and he made that steal, it quite possibly could have been the turning point in the game." I wanted to let other players know they were very important to the team.
>
> ...The star knows he's important and hears it from a variety of sources. You must make sure that others on the team... understand that their role is also very, very important. They should never feel their efforts are wasted in the star's shadow.
>
> It's up to the leader to do that, in sports and elsewhere.[9]

The leader who is serious about service will be quick to recognize the merits of demonstrating appreciation through respect. Consequently, he or she will seize opportunities for exemplifying respect as various situations arise.

For example, I have learned that respect can even be present in situations that involve admonishment. Speaking for myself, I must say that it is never pleasant to be in a position of administering disciplinary action toward another individual. Still, I have tried to make good use of these principles of respect:

1. Even in difficult circumstances, strive to create an initial environment of trust over hostility.
2. Know and follow established parameters.

3. Avoid accusations and innuendos. (It's always best to stay with the facts as you know them.)
4. Keep emotions in check. (This is not to say that you should check-in your emotions –it's okay for certain controlled emotions such as anger to be exerted at appropriate and limited times.)
5. Don't talk down to the individual. (Remember that all of us have our shortcomings.)
6. Communicate genuine care and concern for the person while maintaining the wrongness of the offense.
7. Be fair in rendering judgement. (I have found that "firm when you must and flexible when you may" works well.)
8. Communicate a sense of hope for reconciliation.

Let us move from the example of disapproval and admonishment to one of approval and support. Once again, opportunities for respectful service are present. In this instance, however, our focus is on the leader's knack of demonstrating respect for those under his or her direct supervision. The following guidelines are offered for leaders who wish to respectfully serve those under their authority:

1. Never take someone to task in public.
2. Avoid the disingenuous practice of offering public adulation while speaking adversely of the same person behind his or her back.
3. Show support for those in whom you have invested trust and from whom you have

received loyalty.

4. While it is good to support your most trusted allies, beware of knee-jerk support for everyone under your jurisdiction. (I call this type of blanket support a "circle the wagons" mentality, and have found that it tends to primarily result in defensive posturing as opposed to meeting needs.)
5. Reveal to those under your supervision that you care about them personally. Once again, I believe Coach Wooden's perspective is on target:

   People want to believe you are sincerely interested in them as persons, not just for what they can do for you. You can't fake it. If you don't mean it, they know it—just as you'd know if someone were pretending to be interested in you.

   In the workplace you'll get better cooperation and results if you are sincerely interested in people's families and interests, not simply how they do their job. This will bring productive results. Most people try to live up to expectations.

   It always comes back to courtesy, politeness, and consideration.[10]

While courtesy, politeness, and consideration are certainly expressions of respect, so too is gratitude. A heart felt word of thanks is the icing on the cake of respect.

Now that we have considered empathy, encouragement, facilitation, and appreciation as elements in the process of service, we conclude this chapter with a brief look at certain steps in that process. Each step provides an indication that service is an intentional rather than a fortuitous act.

(1) ***Desire*** *must be present in step one. I believe it is not possible to meet the needs of others without a genuine aspiration for service.*

(2) ***Determination*** *is imperative in step two. One of my favorite selections is the anonymous statement that "a good leader is an ordinary person with extraordinary determination." A great deal of truth exists in those few words regarding both leadership and service.*

(3) ***Opportunity*** *presents itself in step three. Today, opportunities for service range from Boys and Girls Clubs to Senior Centers. In January of 2002, a White House Office for National Service was created in "an effort to kindle national and community service in the wake of the September 11th attacks..."*[11]

(4) ***A Plan of Action*** *gives direction in step four. And while the plan may require occasional adjustments, it may also provide a road map of sorts that can lead to meeting human needs.*

(5) ***Action*** *is the culminating step. Many years ago I ran across this meaningful verse from an unknown author:*

> To look is one thing.
> To see what you look at is
> another.

> To understand what you see is a third.
> To learn from what you.understand is something else.
> But to act on what you have learned is all that matters.

These steps offer a reminder that good intentions alone are of little use when it comes to serving the needs of others. Twelve term Congressman Tony P. Hall, Democrat from Ohio's third district, offers a living example of this truth.

When I had the opportunity to sit down with Congressman Hall in his Capitol Hill office in March of 2002, he had recently been nominated by President Bush to serve as the United States Ambassador and Representative to the United Nations Agencies for Food and Agriculture. A three time nominee for the Nobel Peace Prize, Hall has long been a leading advocate for hunger relief programs and improving international human rights conditions.

Knowing of his prior involvement with the annual National Student Leadership Forum held in Washington, D.C., I began by asking Congressman Hall about the benefits students receive from attending this conference. "...Students get a chance to meet national leaders... They see the hearts of these national leaders... They meet a lot of mentors here. The first thing they learn is that there are a lot of good things going on in D.C. The second thing they learn is that there really are people in D.C. who love the Lord and work bipartisan. The spirit is good during the week. Some say they have the best week they have ever had." He went on to say "The two most important commandments are to love God with all of your heart, soul, and mind and to love others. All of the students are searching. The members of Congress are searching as well."

After congratulating him on his recent appointment, I asked the Congressman what lead him to accept the nomination, and how the new opportunity would tie in with his view of leadership and service." I have served in Congress over 23 years. I wanted to get away from... always thinking about the next campaign. I wanted to devote all of my time in the next few years to serving the poor."

Congressman Hall mentioned that he was not a "Believer" until he came to D.C. "I was more interested in self and ambition. I realized it was false and there had to be more in life. After the first year here I began to look for God. My wife said 'what is the matter with you?' I told her I was hunting for God. I was going to different churches on Sundays. Then a freshman Congressman befriended me and began to speak of Jesus. I knew it was right. I jumped in completely. I did not bring any baggage. One advantage to becoming a Believer later in life is that you do not bring any baggage with you in regards to issues such as doctrine and church. There are more advantages to becoming a Believer younger, but the one advantage to becoming a Believer later in life is this issue of bringing no baggage."

"I have been blessed with good mentors," he continued. "After about three years of being a

Believer, a friend asked what I thought about the idea of bringing Jesus into the workplace." After an initial reluctance to do so, Hall visited Ethiopia in 1984. There he witnessed the tragedy of dying children. Outside of taking care of his district, Hall began to focus on world hunger. "Over and over Jesus talks in the scriptures about hunger." Hall determined that through this issue he could bring the scripture and the Lord into the workplace. Looking forward to his new responsibilities, he said "Being an Ambassador is my ministry."

I concluded my time with Tony Hall by asking him what advice he might offer to young people—at the beginning of a new century—who are interested in serving the needs of their fellow citizens. "Do the thing in front of you. You don't have to necessarily go to other countries. You can go to Dayton, Ohio or St. Louis. Start the work at your school. Get a band together of brothers and sisters and pray together, put your life together. Then the conviction will come because the Holy Spirit is there... Practice what it means to love Jesus... He has a mission for you."

I learned a great deal from Representative Hall that day. I was struck by his vision for combating world hunger. He referred to it as a "spiritual vision" that can manifest itself in "the how." He pointed out that there are a lot of problems in the world, but "hunger—we can lick this one." Beyond his vision, however, I came away from the interview believing that I had spoken to someone who embodies the notion of serving others.

A United States Congressman who had sailed

against the wind of his party by taking a pro-life stance on the issue of abortion;[12] one who had met and interacted with Mother Teresa on five separate occasions; one who had recently been appointed to the rank of Ambassador by the President of the United States; Tony Hall had provided a personification of desire, determination, opportunity, a plan, and action in the honorable pursuit of service.

## ITEMS FOR DISCUSSIONS

1. Discuss the role of empathy in service.
2. Discuss the role of encouragement in service.
3. Discuss the role of facilitation in service.
4. Discuss the role of appreciation in service.
5. Identify and explain a guideline for leaders who wish to respectfully serve those under their authority.

## ENDNOTES


1. Jose Luis Gonzales-Balado, *Mother Teresa In My Own Words* (New York: Gramercy Books, 1996), 23. Permission granted by Liguori Publications.

2. Stephen R. Covey, *Principle-Centered Leadership* (New York: Fireside, 1992), 272.

3. Chris Matthews, *Hardball* (New York: Touch Stone, 1999), 29.

4. Martin H. Manser, *The Westminister Collection of Christian Quotations* (Louisville: Westminster John Knox Press, 2001), 88.

5. Deborah DeFord, Judy Speicher, and Mark LaFlaur, *Reader's Digest Quotable Quotes—Wit and Wisdom For All Occasions From America's Most Popular Magazine* (Pleasantville, NY: The Reader's Digest Association, Inc., 1997), 13. Reprinted with permission from the July 1992 Reader's Digest.

6. David Neidert, *Four Seasons of Leadership* (Provo, UT: Executive Excellence Publishing), 158-159.

7. Reprinted with permission of the publisher. From *The Leadership Wisdom of Jesus—Practical Lesson for Today*, copyright © 1999 by Charles C. Manz, Berrett-Koehler Publishers, Inc., San Francisco, CA. All rights reserved. 1-800-929-2929.

8. Charles C. Manz, *The Leadership Wisdom of Jesus-Practical Lessons for Today* (San Francisco: Berrett-Koehler Publishers, Inc., 1999), 73-74.

9. John Wooden with Steve Jamison, *Wooden—A Lifetime of Observations and Reflections On and Off the Court* (Lincolnwood, IL: Contemporary Books, 1997), 114-115. Material is reproduced with permission of the McGraw Hill Companies.

10. Wooden and Jamison, *Wooden—A Lifetime of Observations and Reflections On and Off the Court*, 139-141.

11. Wooden and Jamison, *Wooden—A Lifetime of Observations and Reflections On and Off the Court*, 33-34.

12. Dana Milbank, "New Director for Faith Based Office," *The Washington Post*, 1 February 2002, A6. Reprinted with permission.

13. Michael Barone with Richard E. Cohen and Founding Editor Grant Ujifusa, *The Almanac of American Politics 2002* (Washington, D.C.: National Journal Group, Inc., 2001), 1199.

# Chapter Seven:

# SERVICE TO SELF

**"Weariness maketh way for wandering."**
**Thomas Manton**

To maintain effectiveness in service, one should be mindful of the need for self-renewal. This sometimes neglected area involves both personal wellness and self-development, each of which are considered in this chapter.

## PERSONAL WELLNESS

The act of giving requires a certain personal constitution. Thus, exhaustion can set in after giving over a period of time. Accordingly, the leader who serves the needs of others must guard against what is typically called "burnout." (I call it giving over and over until there is no "give" to give.)

As noted by Tom Bruno, Jesus was much in tune with this reality of human nature when He walked the earth as both God and man. His human example should speak volumes to those of us who find ourselves swept along by the swift current of contemporary life.

Jesus always retreated before He charged into the battles of life. Before He began the challenge of His ministry, He went into the desert and fasted for forty days, preparing for the difficult days ahead...

Jesus prepared in several ways before He charged into His tasks:

- He used quiet time
- He prayed
- He renewed His faith
- He rested
- He recreated
- He was in constant contact with His Highest Power
- He renewed His mission

> By retreating before He charged, He had the best opportunity for positive results...[1] (Used by kind permission of Bridge-Logos Publishers.)

As leaders intent on serving, we too must be concerned about our personal well-being. Let us therefore consider the adaptability of Bruno's list to our own circumstances.

Having a quiet time alone with God is vital for any Believer, especially one who seeks to lead and serve. I am not one to contend that it has to be a regimented time. (Early in the morning may be great for some, but not for me!) The important thing is to <u>take</u> time to read from God's word and to meditate while being conscious of His presence.

Communion with God through prayer is also essential. If I am going to be instrumental in someone else's life, I want to first seek God's direction.

In renewing our faith, we simultaneously renew ourselves to service. And we do so for the right reasons—not to be caught up in worldly pursuits, but to be faithful to that which God has called us to do.

The old phrase that says "there is no rest for the weary" may be true at times, but it is hardly a badge of honor. I have found that when I am unrested my effectiveness is diminished. Worse than being bad for me, my weariness cheats God from using my service in the fullest manner possible.

There is no question that recreating can be therapeutic. For some this may involve experiencing nature in God's great outdoors. Others may turn to more sedentary activities. In my own case, I find that reading a good biography or following my favorite baseball team (the St. Louis Cardinals) provides necessary compensation. Like anything else, however, leisure can become a vice if it is not used properly. While it may be true that "all work and no play makes Jack a dull boy," it is also true that all play and no work amounts to Jack squat!

Many times I am afraid that Christian men and women fail to call on the power that is at their disposal. When we do in fact call on God's power, it can be quite invigorating. I have no doubt that God wants to empower His children just as a good leader will want to empower his or her followers as discussed in Chapter Four.

Some people believe that to renew themselves requires a monumental change in their lives (for example, a career change). I have fallen into that trap at times only to later learn that it was God's plan to reintroduce me to my current mission. The important thing, I think, is our *willingness* to either follow His leading in a possible new direction or be renewed in our present ambiance.

Bruce Bickel and Stan Jantz have done a masterful job of composing observations that I believe are relevant to personal wellness. I find the following excerpts particularly applicable to those who serve.[2]

**Your Body Is A Temple**

> One of the great mysteries of our culture can be found in our obsession with physical fitness. The mystery isn't that people are exercising more. The mystery is that we're in worse shape than ever.
>
> With the proliferation of fitness clubs, the emphasis on eating healthy foods, and the presence of at least three late-night cable shows dedicated to the latest home exercise apparatus, we should be the fittest people on the planet. Unfortunately, *should* never got anybody into shape. The sad truth is that we are gaining weight at an alarming rate, our children are in terrible shape, and even our professional athletes get beaten by athletes from other countries in any sport we didn't first invent.

What's the problem? We think it has to do with *intention* and *attention.* You probably have every *intention* of getting fit, but you don't. You say you're going to pay *attention* to the details of diet and exercise, but you don't. When you put those two failures together, they spell "out of shape." And out of shape usually leads to all kinds of disadvantages, such as shortness of breath, sleepiness, lack of endurance, and obesity—none of which will add years or quality to your life.

Just like every other area of your life, the secret to getting and staying healthy lies in the details. Change won't happen overnight. It takes time as a multitude of small disciplines are repeated daily. The process may be tedious, but the results are well worth the effort. Not only will you feel better, but you'll think better too! A sound body can enhance a sound mind (conversely, health problems due to sloppy eating habits and sporadic exercise routines can undermine the mind).

We may be spiritual creatures at heart, but while we're on earth our spirits are being housed in our physical bodies. Let's do everything we can to keep the house in top shape.

...IN THE SMALL STUFF

- Fitness of the soul should take priority over fitness of the body, but the two are not mutually exclusive.

- Physical fitness should be a discipline, not an obsession.
- Consistency works better when it's linked to persistency.
- Keep in shape.
- Focus on where you are going rather than where you are.
- It's never too late to make a change in your life.
- You usually lose interest in something that is out of focus.
- When it comes to exercise, direction is more important than speed.
- If you start your day with the expectation that nothing meaningful will occur, you won't be disappointed.
- Do it now.
- What you get out of your body relates directly to what you put in it.
- Don't run with the ball unless you know the direction of the goal.
- Your biggest success will be in striving to be the best you can be, and only you can succeed at that.
- Don't go for fad diets. You may lose weight in the short term, but in the long run the only thing getting slimmer will be your wallet.
- A healthy body and a sharp mind usually go together.

- Run the race to win, even if you don't have a chance.

### Stop Worrying and Start Living

Worrying is one of the most destructive of all human habits because it decreases your effectiveness in other areas. When you worry about something, your thoughts and your emotions focus on events that haven't yet taken place. It's like Mark Twain once said: "I am an old man and have known a great many troubles, but most of them have never happened."

Worrying is totally passive. It accomplishes nothing. On the other hand, worrying can literally make you sick while keeping you from accomplishing the things that really matter. Here's a sobering thought: Worry can keep you from living your life the way God intended it. Think about the things you worry about. Amazingly, you probably worry about the small stuff. Those details of life over which you have little or no control. Oswald Chambers wrote: "It is not only wrong to worry, it is unbelief; worrying means we do not believe that God can look after the practical details of our lives, and it is never anything but those details that worry us."

... Are you trying to arrange the details of your life so carefully that you are leaving God out of the process? Then you're probably worrying too much. You're relying on your own abilities, and you think you have a lot to lose if things don't turn out the way you want.

Clearly, the antidote to worry is trusting God to

take care of the small stuff in your life...

... IN THE SMALL STUFF

- Live longer by worrying less.
- Don't worry about what you can't do. If you must worry, worry about why you won't do what you should do.
- Before you worry needlessly, ask yourself, "What's the worst thing that can happen?"
- When you're feeling overwhelmed, remember to take things one at a time—one day at a time.
- Worrying occurs when God is left out of the process.
- Anxiety is short lived if we give it to God.
- If you prepare for the future you won't have to worry about it.
- Don't worry as much about where you are as where you are going.
- Rather than worrying about change, learn to thrive on it.
- Worry is a choice.
- When you choose to worry, you are choosing not to trust God.
- Worrying can literally harm you—emotionally, physically, mentally, and spiritually.
- Instead of worrying about what you can't do, think about what God can do for you.

- The best way to stop worrying is to start praying.
- Never confuse worrying about tomorrow with planning for tomorrow.
- Prayer changes things; worry changes nothing.

Before we move on from the topic of personal wellness, one additional thought bears mentioning. Don't feel guilty about the matter of self-care. As noted by Parker Palmer:

> ... Self-care is never a selfish act—it is simply good stewardship of the only gift I have, the gift I was put on earth to offer to others. Anytime we can listen to true self and give it the care it requires, we do so not only for ourselves but for the many others whose lives we touch.[3]

## SELF DEVELOPMENT

In concluding this chapter, we look at self development as a contributing part of self-renewal. Rick Lynch and Sue Vineyard point out sixteen ways to further one's self-development.[4]

> Leaders work hard at their own self-development. They are never satisfied with the "status quo" in their organizations or in their own development. They have a burning desire to grow, to learn, to improve themselves and therefore do the following:
>
> 1. Attend seminars.

2. Read widely and diversely,
    a. Subscribe to professional journals
    b. Examine periodicals that offer different perspectives on issues.
    c. Learn the historical perspective of groups and issues.
3. Take continuing education and advanced degree classes at college.
4. Seek out interesting and enlightening people.
5. Belong to professional organizations and attend their meetings.
6. Seek to understand varied points of view (understanding does not mean agreement).
7. Be open to new ideas.
8. "Play" with ideas.
9. Challenge orthodoxy.
10. Avoid safe "ruts."
11. Ask Questions.
12. Make wellness of self a priority.
13. Examine previous conclusions for current appropriateness.
14. Learn from mistakes—then let them go.
15. Look for learning in every encounter and event.
16. Keep listening after hearing something that is different or even offensive.

The leader who strives to serve the needs of others will recognize the value of some type of ongoing personal development. When a leader pays attention to this area, it is those he or she serves who stand to benefit.

## ITEMS FOR DISCUSSIONS

1. Discuss this statement: To maintain effectiveness in service, one should be mindful of the need for self-renewal.
2. Explain how renewing faith can renew the ability to serve.
3. Discuss the role of physical fitness in self-renewal.
4. Explain how worry can decrease effectiveness in service.
5. Identify and discuss one particular way in which the leader may attend to self-development.

## ENDNOTES

1. Tom Bruno, *Jesus Ph.D. Psychologist* (Gainesville, Florida: Bridge-Logos Publishers, 2000), 144.

2. Bruce Bickel and Stan Jantz, *God Is In The Small Stuff—And It All Matters* (Uhrichsville, Ohio: Promise Press, an imprint of Barbour Publishing, Inc. 1998), 95-99, 119-123. Used by permission.

3. Parker J. Palmer, *Let Your Life Speak—Listening For The Voice of Vocation* (San Francisco: Jossey—Bass Inc., 2000), 30-31. Reprinted by permission of John Wiley & Sons, Inc.

4. Rick Lynch and Sue Vineyard, *Secrets of Leadership* (Downers Grove, Illinois: Heritage Arts Publishing, 1991), 74.

# Chapter Eight:

# THE CREDIBILITY FACTOR IN SERVICE

**"We make our decisions and then our decisions turn around and make us."**
**Francis William (F.W.) Boreham**

This chapter explores how the leader is able to achieve and maintain credibility with those he or she serves. More precisely, it addresses the issue of credibility from the standpoints of character and accountability.

## CREDIBILITY AND CHARACTER

In leadership and service, credibility may be viewed as a natural outgrowth of character. Simply put, an individual with high character will have strong credibility with those he or she serves. Conversely, credibility will be in short supply if character is found lacking.

Most leaders—like most people in general—are

protective of their reputations. However, reputation is actually a side issue. Character is what matters. Dr. D.L. Moody puts it in perspective with these insightful words: "If I take care of my character, my reputation will take care of itself."[1]

Let us therefore consider how character makes a difference in leadership and service. The leader who wants to keep his or her credibility intact, may go a long way toward that end by taking this list to heart:

1. Character strives to uphold truth;
   A lack of character thinks nothing of blurring the truth.
2. Character declares if it is wrong, it is unacceptable;
   A lack of character claims it is wrong only if you get caught.
3. Character declares that public thoughts and actions should reflect private lifestyle;
   A lack of character claims that public life and private life are two separate matters.
4. Character makes ethical behavior a priority;
   A lack of character ridicules ethical standards as sanctimonious and intolerant.
5. Character declares that problems are to be dealt with;
   A lack of character is inclined to look the other way.
6. Character seeks justice;
   A lack of character seeks justice—only for others.
7. Character takes an unpopular stand when necessary;

A lack of character punts.

8. Character stands up for principle;
   A lack of character asks "what is principle?"
9. Character declares it is how you react to personal adversity that matters;
   A lack of character bemoans the unfairness of personal adversity.
10. Character considers others;
    A lack of character looks out for number one.
11. Character is intent on setting a good example;
    A lack of character claims "what I do is nobody else's business."
12. Character seeks to motivate others;
    A lack of character seeks to manipulate others.
13. Character is unpretentious;
    A lack of character is quick to usurp.
14. Character predetermines how to react to temptation;
    A lack of character reacts to temptation as situations arise.
15. Character declares that one should act responsibly;
    A lack of character claims "if it feels good, do it."
16. Character accepts responsibility for words and actions;
    A lack of character makes excuses.
17. Character finds time to serve;
    A lack of character routinely claims "Let

someone else do it."

## CREDIBILITY AND ACCOUNTABILITY

In recent years, accountability has become a popular concept in certain circles. The idea of being in an "accountability group" or having an "accountability partner" seems to have some appeal. This is not, however, the kind of accountability addressed in this chapter. Instead, in the context of leadership and service, personal accountability is a matter of holding oneself accountable for words and actions.

In the events leading up to the impeachment of President Clinton in 1998-99, personal accountability was a practice that was sorely missing. Had the President been able to demonstrate personal accountability, he could have saved himself and the nation a great deal of pain.

On December 19, 1998, Congressman J. C. Watts of Oklahoma rose to speak on the floor of the United States House of Representatives. In his speech explaining why he would vote in favor of articles of impeachment, Congressman Watts made the case for personal accountability as an example for children. Said the Congressman:

> Mr. Speaker, there is no joy sometimes in upholding the law. It is so unpleasant sometimes that we hire other people to do it for us. Ask the police or judges. It is tiring and thankless. But we know it must be done, because if we do not point at lawlessness, our children cannot see it. If we do not label lawlessness, our children cannot rec-

ognize it. And if we do not punish lawlessness, our children will not believe it.

So if someone were to ask me, 'J.C., why did you vote for the articles of impeachment?' I would say I did it for our children. How can we tell our children that honesty is the best policy if we do not demand honesty as a policy? How can we expect a Boy Scout to honor his oath if elected officials do not honor theirs? How can we expect a business executive to honor a promise when the chief executive abandons his or hers?

Whether it is a promise or a truth or a vow or an oath, a person's word is the firm footing our society stands upon, and the average kid understands that. They do not need a grand jury to enforce it. They say 'cross your heart, hope to die'; 'pinkie promise'; 'king's X'; 'blood brother.' These are the childhood instincts that seek to draw a line between the honest and the dishonest, between the principled and the unprincipled.

Ask the children. The kid who lies does not last and they do not bicker over what is and what is not a lie. They know. So do I. So do the American people.

Time and again, we wanted the essence of truth and we got the edges of the truth. We hear, 'Let's get on with the business of our country.' What business is

> more important than teaching our children right from wrong? Some say it is all about politics and party lines. If that were true, I would have given in to popular opinion. But what is popular is not always what is right.
>
> Some say polls are against this. Polls measure changing feelings, not steadfast principle. Polls would have rejected the Ten Commandments. Polls would have embraced slavery and ridiculed women's rights.
>
> Some say we must draw this to a close. I say we must draw a line between right and wrong; not with a tiny fine line of an executive fountain pen, but with the big, thick lead of a Number 2 pencil. We must do it so every kid in America can see it.
>
> The point is not whether the President can prevail, but whether truth can prevail. We need to cease the cannibalizing of Members of Congress. We need to cease the attacks on the President of the United States. His is not the injured party. Our country is.
>
> In this moment, our children's future is more important than our future. If our country looks the other way, our country will lose its way.[2]

To perpetuate credibility, the leader must avoid the lure of playing games with right and wrong. Hence, credibility in service calls for the kind of personal accountability that will steer clear of "games" such as these:

1. The Game of Denial
2. The Prove It Game
3. Word Games
4. The Change the Subject Game
5. The Game of So What?
6. The "I didn't Intend" Game
7. The Blame Game
8. The Vilification Game
9. The Mercy Over Consequences Game

## THE GAME OF DENIAL

The game involving denial is mentioned first due to the fact that it is often a first response of one who is running from accountability. Unfortunately, the leader is not immune from the possible use of this tactic of deny, deny, deny.

When a leader slips into a state of denial, he or she is just digging a deeper hole. Therefore, it is important (not to mention ethical) for the leader to quickly acknowledge mistakes.

## THE PROVE IT GAME

Those of us who cherish American values are likely to agree that "innocent until proven guilty" is a proper legal edict to follow. However, apart from a legal context, it has become all too common for people to claim this notion as a means for avoiding personal accountability.

A leader who strives for credibility among those

he or she serves, must recognize the need for transparency. Thus the question for the leader is not one of proof of behavior. Rather it is one of taking responsibility for behavior.

## WORD GAMES

If denial or evidence of proof are not advantageous, word games sometimes become an alternative tactic for some who would resist personal accountability. This strategy is, I believe, unacceptable for a responsible leader.

Parsing words (such as debating the meaning of the word "is") is beneath the dignity of one who leads others. In making use of this technique the leader risks the possibility—at some point—of not being taken seriously.

## THE CHANGE THE SUBJECT GAME

When cornered as a result of their own inappropriate words or actions, some try to change the subject. While this procedure may work in the short run, its life is usually short lived.

National leaders have at times used this approach. During periods of personal crisis, they and their cohorts have stressed the need to focus on the more "important" issues of the day, such as the economy or foreign policy. Again, the leader should identify with a higher standard if credibility is to be maintained. And what is that higher standard? I believe it is to opt for personal accountability, rather than playing games such as The Change The Subject Game.

## THE GAME OF SO WHAT?

Personal accountability is far more desirable for the leader than is participation in the game of so what? In this game, attitude is used as a self-defense. Comments such as these are common: "So what? It's no big deal;" "So what? Everybody does it;" "So what? It's nobody's business but mine."

In each of these statements, personal accountability is nowhere to be found. Clearly, it is best for leaders who serve others to take a higher road.

## THE "I DIDN'T INTEND" GAME

The "I didn't intend" game is a calculated mind game that acknowledges error while maintaining pure motivation. In this game the guilty party succeeds if he or she can convince others that no harm was meant.

More often than not, the individual who plays this game is looking for an easy way out. My experience has taught me that it is best—for the sake of accountability—to stick to the real issue as opposed to getting side tracked on the questions of intentions.

## THE BLAME GAME

From the time that Adam first blamed Eve for his disobedience (and Eve blamed the serpent) The Blame Game has been a human pastime. The leader is just as likely as his or her followers to get caught up in passing on blame. Bob Goddard says it well: "To err is human; to blame it on the other guy is even more human."[3]

If the leader is serious about maintaining credibility, he or she will resist the temptation to join in this game. An admirable leader will take responsibility when he or she falls short of the mark.

## THE VILIFICATION GAME

Essentially, vilification is an advanced version of the Blame Game. In this case, however, other individuals are not only blamed, they are discredited. Essentially the idea is to take the spotlight off of one in favor of shining it elsewhere. If this is done successfully, it results in someone else becoming the target.

During the months surrounding the impeachment of President Clinton, the vilification game was much in evidence. If it wasn't those involved in a so called "vast right wing conspiracy," it was Independent Counsel Kenneth Starr who was singled out for vilification by the President and his operatives. (And I must say that their strategy met with some success.)

However, we should ask ourselves, is this the kind of leadership and service that is worthy of followship? I think not.

## THE MERCY OVER CONSEQUENCES GAME

I have observed that some are quite good at this game. The idea is to acknowledge shortcomings, ask for forgiveness, and hope that the matter will go away.

That is all well and good except for one thing. Consequences are <u>not</u> optional. Depending on the nature of the circumstance, the consequences may be great or small. But there will be consequences (some of which may be on-going).

Charles W. Colson is a case-in-point. Having paid the high price of going to jail as a result of his involvement in the Watergate scandal of the 1970s, Colson now leads a productive life. Speaking of the change that took place in his life, Colson's perspective bears mentioning. In his own words, Colson explains "Conversion may occur in an instant, but the process of coming from sinfulness into a new life can be a long and arduous journey."[4] Colson is to be admired for making that journey.

Hopefully, the leader will be able to avoid the kinds of situations that call for serious repercussions. However, it is important to remember that mercy does not negate consequences. Bill Bennett provides an additional perspective.

The attempts to use God's forgiveness as a pretext to excuse moral wrong is a dangerous (and old) heresy known as antinomianism—literally "against the law." Essentially it rejects the moral law as a relevant part of Christian experience. The thought that God's grace, given to us through Christ's death at Galgotha, would justify licentiousness has long been considered contemptible by saints and scholars through the ages. And rightly so. ...Forgiveness is becoming a synonym for lax standards and tolerance for (and acceptance of) transgressions. And that is a terrible thing to allow to happen. For in Christian doctrine, forgiveness comes at an extraordinarily high cost...

We violate God's canons of justice when we

invoke forgiveness casually, trivially, promiscuously. And even in those moments when forgiveness is given properly—and such moments of "costly grace" can be an extraordinary witness to the world—the person forgiven should *still* be held accountable for his acts. We reap what we sow—even when there is contrition.[5]

The leader who serves others must, I believe, strive to preserve personal credibility by maintaining character and accountability. In so doing, the leader helps others, makes a positive contribution to the cultural environment, and helps secure a personal legacy of service.

## ITEMS FOR DISCUSSION

1. Explain how character and credibility are connected.
2. Discuss the fact that reputation is a side issue with respect to credibility and character.
3. Explain the role of accountability in achieving and maintaining credibility.
4. Explain the "game of so what?"
5. Discuss how the "vilification game" is an extension of the "blame game."

## ENDNOTES

1. Martin H. Manser, *The Westminster Collection of Christian Quotations* (Louisville: (Westminster John Knox Press, 2001), 32.

2. J.C. Watts, "H11968 Privileges of the House—Impeaching William Jefferson Clinton, President of the United States, for High Crimes and Misdemeanors; Congressional Record — House of Representatives; Proceedings and Debates of the 105th Congress, Second Session; Washington, D.C., Saturday, December 19, 1998."

3. Deborah De Ford, Judy Speicher, and Mark La Flaur, *Readers' Digest Quotable Quotes: Wit and Wisdom For All Occasions From America's Most Popular Magazine* (Pleasantville, New York: The Readers' Digest Association, Inc. 1997), 68.

4. Martin H. Manser, *The Westminster Collection of Christian Quotations*, 52.

5. William J. Bennett, *The Death of Outrage—Bill Clinton and the Assult on American Ideals* (New York: The Free Press, Copyright © 1998 by William J. Bennett ), 117-119. Reprinted with permission of the Free Press, an imprint of Simon & Schuster Trade Publishing Group.

# POSTSCRIPT

A premise of the preceding chapters is that a valid relationship exists between one's potential to serve well and lead effectively. Thus, this final segment offers an inclusive personal charge. May the nuggets included in this charge help stimulate the thoughts and actions of those who choose to lead and serve.

**L**ove both God and your neighbor.
**E**volve as a leader. (It takes time.)
**A**spire to be part of something bigger than yourself.
**D**are to fail so that you may succeed.

And

**S**hare your talents and abilities. (That's why God gave them to you.)
**E**arn the respect of those you serve.
**R**emember that your decisions impact others.
**V**est your life in the lives of others.
**E**ntrust yourself to God.

## LOVE BOTH GOD AND YOUR NEIGHBOR

Although we can never demonstrate our love for God in the same way He has demonstrated His love for us, we must recognize that fulfilling the command to love God is essential. I believe it is not going too far to suggest that attempting to lead and serve while ignoring this greatest commandment is tantamount to an exercise in futility.

The initial emphasis on loving God should naturally progress to include others. Indeed, loving others exhibits a love for God.

I have never subscribed to the notion that the focus of a Christian's love for God should begin and end with suffusive involvement in things like group Bible studies, praise and worship events, and listening to Christian music. Lest I be misunderstood, I must hasten to point out that these are worthy pursuits. However, it seems to me that there is something wrong with that picture if it fails to reflect the needs of others.

## EVOLVE AS A LEADER (IT TAKES TIME)

While I trust that the material contained in the preceding chapters is of utilitarian value, its application will necessarily develop over time. Many factors are likely to precipitate practical application. I will mention three that tend to be prominent.

First, I am convinced that God brings people into our lives at specific times for specific purposes. Having observed this reality in my own life, I have noticed that it is a two way street. I am grateful that I have been given the privilege of impacting the lives of others. I am also thankful for certain special individuals who have impacted my life.

In addition to people, education is a key factor. It is important to be mindful of ways in which formal training lends itself to developing a capacity for leadership and service, both presently and with respect to future endeavors.

Finally, the personal circumstances of life (both good and bad) provide a developmental laboratory. Whether it involves moving forward with an exciting prospect or contending with a difficult situation, our circumstances and the application of leadership and service are often germane to each other.

## ASPIRE TO BE PART OF SOMETHING BIGGER THAN YOURSELF

A person who leads primarily for self-serving purposes is, I believe, unworthy of his or her followers. Therefore it is critical to get outside of yourself.

Although there are many great causes, consideration should be given to more than the cause itself. At least two other considerations should guide our minds and hearts.

First, is the cause a good fit for you? I have become a soft touch when it comes to household pets. In recent years I have surprisingly developed a fondness for cats. (I like dogs too.) But not withstanding this affection, I would be uncomfortable affiliating with certain animal rights groups. A similar contention can be made regarding other issues. (The environment is one that comes to mind.) Conversely, I am pleased to be involved in Christian higher education. Thus it is important to know and be comfortable with your affiliations. This will help ensure a good fit, and you will be more apt to devote yourself to a cause you can fully endorse.

Beyond the right fit, however, lies another basic issue for those who lead and serve. When it comes to personal involvement in anything (job, church, community, etc.) we are often caught up in the "what." For example, we seem to pay a lot of attention to job title, job description, and the like. However, if we are serious about being part something bigger than ourselves, we need to consider that the "why" is generally more significant than the "what." As a telling example, I cite the crucifixion of Christ. *What* He did for us on that first Good Friday, as excruciating as it must have been, pales in significance when we consider *why* he paid that awful price.

Thus, the "why" deserves our attention. In aspiring to be part of something bigger than ourselves, we should not neglect this vital consideration.

## DARE TO FAIL SO THAT YOU MAY SUCCEED

Some people dare to be cautious. They often appear driven by a fear of failure. Others seem willing to throw caution to the wind. I find defects in both of the aforementioned positions. The best approach, I believe, lies somewhere in between. The leader who is intent on serving should be ready to seize the moment, but only when the moment is right.

Seize the moment! This bold directive should not

be taken lightly. Minus a predisposition to step up to the plate, you are apt to fall into one of two categories. Either you will not be on the lookout for your "moment" and it will come and go without your knowledge, or timidity and reluctance will regularly prevail when opportunity knocks.

While I believe that seizing the moment makes sense, I also contend that it is crucial to do so only when the time is right for you. How can you know when the time is right? That question may be addressed by pondering self-imposed questions such as: Am I fully prepared for this moment? Have I weighed all of my options? Do I have an objective grasp of the identifiable pros and cons? What are the ramifications for myself and others? Do I have political capital to spend? Am I willing to live with certain outcomes? Most importantly, and after making it a matter of prayer, what is my sense of God's direction?

I maintain that folks who are reluctant to seize the moment are more likely to be followers than candidates for leadership and service. For those who *are* inclined to lead and serve, my advice is be ready to seize your moment!

## SHARE YOUR TALENTS AND ABILITIES (THAT'S WHY GOD GAVE THEM TO YOU)

In family circles, we know it is not unusual for children to inherit certain characteristics from their parents. Still, one child can be—and often is—very different from another.

As God's children created in His image, we

inherit certain characteristics from our Heavenly Father (the ability to love, for example). Yet, we too are different when it comes to individual talents and abilities. Some inherit God's knack for creativity (to a smaller degree of course). Some possess physical talents and abilities while others are more cerebral.

Those who lead and serve should make conscious use of their God-given talents and abilities. By combining natural skills with the learned concepts and practices described in the preceding chapters, the potential for being instrumental in the lives of others is enhanced.

## EARN THE RESPECT OF THOSE YOU SERVE

In Chapter Six, respect is discussed in relation to appreciation. We must remind ourselves, however, that respect is not automatic. It must be earned. The following guidelines provide a formula for earning respect in leadership and service.

First, be genuine. It is difficult to respect someone who is less than authentic. That is one reason why *Leadership, Not Salesmanship* was chosen as the primary title for this book. The idea is not for you to take on a persuasive character that will somehow convince people to purchase a bill of goods. Instead, you must be yourself. To be *real* effective in leadership and service, you must begin by being *real.*

Second, take the initiative. Don"t wait until others show you respect. Take it upon yourself to show others how it is done. Though there will be exceptions to this rule, you will generally find that the practice of being respectful toward others will be returned in kind.

Third, have the best interests of those you lead and serve at heart. Don't expect much in the way of respect if people believe that you have *your* interests at heart. Make an effort to let them know you care about *their* concerns.

Fourth and last, strive to build sincere personal regard for and from those you lead and serve. When this is done properly, respect will be of such magnitude that letting the other one down becomes a worst nightmare scenario, and <u>not</u> letting each other down is the regular order of the day.

## REMEMBER THAT YOUR DECISIONS IMPACT OTHERS

In October of 2001, The Board of Trustees for the university where I am employed approved a six month sabbatical leave for me from January 1, 2002 through June 30, 2002. It was during that time that I moved to the Washington, D.C. area and did most of the writing contained in this book.

While living in the shadow of our nation's capital, I found myself considering the possibility of pursuing a new opportunity for service. In considering this option, I soon realized that my decision would impact people other than myself. I was particularly aware of the fact that timing would be of utmost concern. When it came time to decide whether to move forward in this consideration, I was informed that an additional waiting period of weeks would be necessary. At that point, I realized I would not be comfortable keeping my family, my staff, the students, the university president, or the Board of Trustees (that had so graciously granted my leave in the first place) waiting for an extended period of time on an impending decision.

I share this personal story to emphasize something that should have been obvious to me from the beginning. Decisions are not made in a vacuum. Major decisions with ramifications for others should be considerate of others. Although I admit there was some initial interest on my part in contemplating the prospect of a new service opportunity, the timing was not right and I felt immediate affirmation when I communicated that I would be returning to the university.

As leaders who serve, we must always remember to consider others in our decisions. That is not to say that our decisions will always please others. It is, however, another way to practice the spirit of the principles and guidelines described in this book.

## VEST YOUR LIFE IN THE LIVES OF OTHERS

From time to time we hear that someone has a "vested interest" in other persons or things. This means that the individual with a "vested interest" has devoted resources—typically time, energy, and finances—to someone or something in particular.

Motive is of critical importance when it comes to vesting your life in the lives of others. I will share a negative example followed by a positive example in order to highlight its significance.

Parents who seem to want to live vicariously through their children appear motivated by all of the wrong reasons. Rather than just letting their kids be kids, they sometimes push and push to the point of making what should be an enjoyable activity (summer baseball and softball programs, varsity cheerleading, the list goes on and on) anything but fun. They may have a vested interest but, the truth be known, they are more likely motivated by their own agenda than by the wishes of their children. I must quickly point out that many parents do in fact allow their children to enjoy their activities rather than trying to use their kids as a way to revisit their own childhood. These parents deserve accolades for their efforts to keep things in a proper perspective.

On a more positive note is a mentoring program of which I am familiar. Dr. Renee Waters is Associate Professor of Music at Southwest Baptist University in Bolivar, Missouri. Originally Dr. Waters started the Student to Student Mentoring program for the purpose of addressing the issue of student retention. The idea calls for upperclassmen to serve as mentors for freshmen. The program is well conceived and was initiated in part to address a shortage of tutors. To the pleasant surprise of those monitoring the program, it has been found to have a positive impact on upperclassmen as well as freshmen. By serving as mentors, non-freshmen have discovered strengths of which they were previously unaware. The Student to Student Mentoring program is a good example of how we can personally benefit from vesting our lives in the lives of others.

## ENTRUST YOURSELF TO GOD

Now it is time for true confession. I would be less than candid if I did not admit that I struggle with this final charge. Consequently, I am addressing myself at least as much as others. The good news is that I can report some slow but sure improvement on my part. As they say, I am a "work in progress."

As a Christian involved in leadership and service, I have had to come to grips with an important reality. No matter how effective I may or may not be, God is ultimately in charge. It should be a relief to know that I can entrust myself to God, do my part in leading and serving, and leave the results to Him. (When I am able to do that is when I feel most at peace.) But notwithstanding my best intentions, I often seem to want to do more than my part. It is as if I have to make sure that God is following through on certain things (a wrong-headed thought to say the least).

I have found, however, that the more I am able to entrust myself to God, the more He honors my leadership and service. I am not a theologian, but I sense that God is more concerned with our willingness to give ourselves over to Him than He is with the details of our efforts on His behalf.

It seems fitting to close on this note. May God honor our leadership and service as we make headway in entrusting ourselves to Him.

# ENDNOTES FOR CHAPTER TITLE QUOTATIONS

**Chapter One: GRASPING THE CONCEPT OF LEADERSHIP**
Martin H. Manser, *The Westminster Collection of Christian Quotations* (Louisville: Westminster John Knox Press, 2001), 228.

**Chapter Two: THE LEADER**
Robert G. Torricelli, *Quotations for Public Speakers—A Historical, Literary, and Political Anthology* (New Brunswick: Rutgers University Press, 2001), 158.

**Chapter Three: THE VISION**
Deborah Deford, Judy Speicher, and Mark LaFlaur, *Readers' Digest Quotable Quotes—Wit and Wisdom for All Occasions from America's Most Popular Magazine* (Pleasantville, New York: The Readers' Digest Association, Inc., 1997), 19.

**Chapter Four: IMPLEMENTING THE VISION**
Martin H. Manser, *The Westminster Collection of Christian Quotations*, 2.

**Chapter Five: SELFLESSNESS AND SERVICE**
Martin H. Manser, *The Westminster Collection of Christian Quotations*, 388.

**Chapter Six: THE PROCESS OF SERVING OTHERS**
Martin H. Manser, *The Westminster Collection of Christian Quotations*, 122.

**Chapter Seven: SERVICE TO SELF**
Martin H. Manser, *The Westminster Collection of Christian Quotations*, 378.

**Chapter Eight: THE CREDIBILITY FACTOR IN SERVICE**
Martin H. Manser, *The Westminster Collection of Christian Quotations*, 65.

# APPENDIX A

# Measuring Fundamental Political Beliefs

The following instrument is designed to help the leader identify his or her personal political disposition.

Circle the response that best describes your position on the issues.

1. The United States should move forward aggressively in developing a high-tech protective nuclear defense shield.

Strongly Agree   Agree   Disagree   Strongly Disagree

2. It is not a good idea for the U.S. to withdraw from the Anti Ballistic Missile (ABM) Treaty signed with the Soviet Union in the 1970s.

Strongly Agree   Agree   Disagree   Strongly Disagree

3. The current level of spending on national defense should be increased.

Strongly Agree Agree Disagree Strongly Disagree

4. Human rights violations should not be a factor in U.S.–China relations.

Strongly Agree Agree Disagree Strongly Disagree

5. The U.S. should take a pro-active approach in dealing with known terrorists around the world.

Strongly Agree Agree Disagree Strongly Disagree

6. Non-U.S. citizens from the middle east with visa violations should not be systematically detained for questioning in relationship to the war on terrorism.

Strongly Agree Agree Disagree Strongly Disagree

7. In the war on terrorism, the U.S. should maintain the option of invoking a military court for non-U.S. citizens charged with war-related crimes.

Strongly Agree Agree Disagree Strongly Disagree

8. The end of the Cold War had little to do with the U.S. military build-up of the 1980s.

Strongly Agree Agree Disagree Strongly Disagree

9. If at all possible, pro-life judges should be appointed to the Supreme Court when vacancies occur.

Strongly Agree   Agree   Disagree   Strongly Disagree

10. Partial-birth abortion is a morally acceptable medical procedure.

Strongly Agree   Agree   Disagree   Strongly Disagree

11. Stricter gun control laws in the U.S. would not have a significant impact on reducing violent crime.

Strongly Agree   Agree   Disagree   Strongly Disagree

12. The death penalty should be outlawed in the U.S. as a form of punishment for violent crime.

Strongly Agree   Agree   Disagree   Strongly Disagree

13. Lying under oath should be considered an impeachable offense for public officials.

Strongly Agree   Agree   Disagree   Strongly Disagree

14. Educational vouchers should not be an option for children attending public schools.

Strongly Agree Agree Disagree Strongly Disagree

15. Hate crime legislation is unnecessary given existing laws in the U.S.

Strongly Agree Agree Disagree Strongly Disagree

16. National health care should be provided by the federal government for all U.S. citizens.

Strongly Agree Agree Disagree Strongly Disagree

17. Campaign finance reform should place equal restrictions on unions and corporations.

Strongly Agree Agree Disagree Strongly Disagree

18. Tax cuts for American taxpayers should be targeted according to levels of income.

Strongly Agree Agree Disagree Strongly Disagree

19. Tax breaks for both small businesses and large corporations help fuel the national economy.

Strongly Agree Agree Disagree Strongly Disagree

20. When a federal budget surplus exists, the surplus should be spent on government programs.

Strongly Agree Agree Disagree Strongly Disagree

21. Raising the minimum wage does more harm that good for the American economy.

Strongly Agree Agree Disagree Strongly Disagree

22. Annual spending for domestic social programs in the U.S. should increase systematically.

Strongly Agree Agree Disagree Strongly Disagree

23. Lawmakers should make it possible for U.S. citizens to opt for a private retirement plan in lieu of paying into social security.

Strongly Agree Agree Disagree Strongly Disagree

24. Affirmative action is necessary to ensure fair hiring practices.

Strongly Agree Agree Disagree Strongly Disagree

## Measuring Fundamental Political Beliefs (Key)

Odd numbers should be scored as follows:

Strongly Agree = 4
Agree = 3
Disagree = 2
Strongly Disagree = 1

Even numbers should be scored as follows:

Strongly Agree = 1
Agree = 2
Disagree = 3
Strongly Disagree = 4

Add totals and assign to corresponding location on chart. The number on the chart that is closest to the total score, indicates the overall political leaning of the individual completing the questionnaire.

**Personal Chart For Measuring Fundamental Political Beliefs**

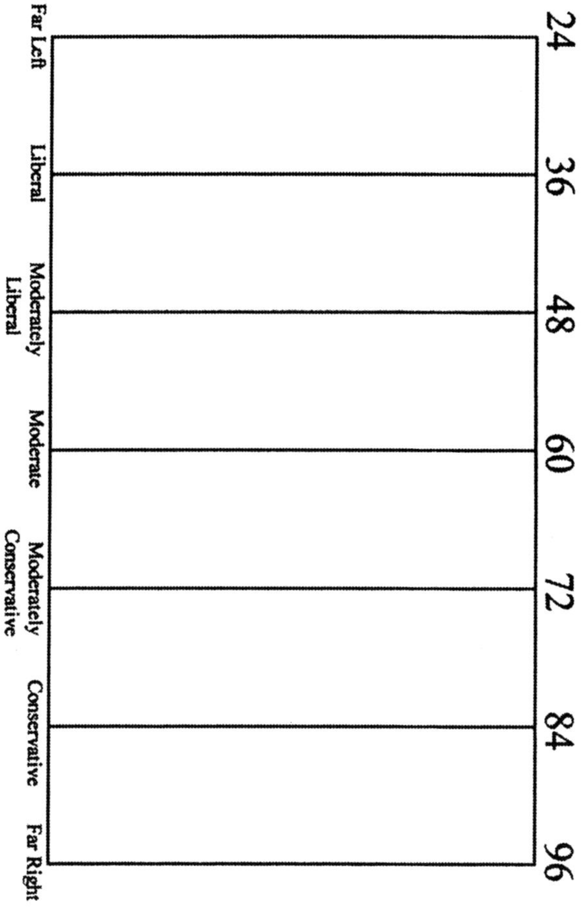

## APPENDIX B

# TEXT EXAMINATION

The instrument that follows is designed to evaluate knowledge of material included in Chapters One through Eight. Instructors who wish to use this examination—for the purpose of academic testing—may secure an answer key by sending a request to the address below:

The Roy Blunt Service and Leadership Training Program
Office of Student Life
Southwest Baptist University
1600 University Avenue
Bolivar, Missouri 65613

(Please note that the request must be on official letterhead, and must be accompanied by a self-addressed stamped envelop.)

Instructions for completing the examination:

Place a checkmark in the space provided next to the letter (A, B, C, or D) that most accurately corresponds to the numerically identified question or statement.

1. Which of the following phrases describe leadership?
   ____A. The focus is the process.
   ____B. The focus is the product.
   ____C. The focus is efficiency.
   ____D. All of the above.

2. Which of the following statements is <u>not</u> true?
   ____A. Leadership is a learned art.
   ____B. Leadership requires a forward-looking mentality.
   ____C. Leadership requires political prowess.
   ____D. Leadership and management are essentially the same.

3. The term that best defines leadership is:
   ____A. Influence.
   ____B. Power.
   ____C. Administration.
   ____D. Authority.

4. An effective leader is able to:
 ____A. Be all things to all people.
 ____B. Balance core convictions with pragmatic decision making.
 ____C. Be firm at all times.
 ____D. Be driven by pragmatic instincts.

5. Which of the following descriptions summarize that which draws people to the leader?
 ____A. Someone who does not rock the boat.
 ____B. Someone who appears larger than life.
 ____C. Someone who can offer a sense of that which may be.
 ____D. Someone who can offer an unusually high degree of intelligence.

6. What leadership trait(s) did Presidents Franklin Roosevelt and Ronald Reagan have in common?
 ____A. The ability to provide a sense of hope.
 ____B. Impeccable personal lifestyles.
 ____C. Similar ideological views on most issues.
 ____D. All of the above.

7. What personal characteristic do people most admire in a leader?
    ____A. Decisive.
    ____B. Honest.
    ____C. Intelligent.
    ____D. Broad-minded.

8. Which of the following statements apply to vision?
    ____A. Only leaders with healthy motives can be visionaries.
    ____B. The leader will display a noble vision only.
    ____C. The leader will display a workable vision only.
    ____D. The leader will display a noble vision and a workable vision.

9. Which of the following do people initially buy into?
    ____A. The leader.
    ____B. The noble vision.
    ____C. The workable vision.
    ____D. Both B and C.

10. The "super conscious mind" reflects:
    ____A. Vision rooted in conviction.
    ____B. Vision rooted in a dream.
    ____C. Vision rooted in a personal circumstance.
    ____D. Vision rooted in an idea.

11. The vision for Empower America was implemented:
    ____A. At the beginning of the Reagan Administration.
    ____B. At the end of the Reagan Administration.
    ____C. At the beginning of the Clinton Administration.
    ____D. At the end of the Clinton Administration.
12. A vision rooted in an ideal:
    ____A. Is broad in scope.
    ____B. Is narrow in scope.
    ____C. Is the same as vision rooted in an idea.
    ____D. Is the same as vision rooted in conviction.

13. Bill O'Reilly speaks of Robert Kennedy and his vision:
    ____A. In favorable terms.
    ____B. In unfavorable terms.
    ____C. In apathetic terms.
    ____D. In uncertain terms.

14. President Kennedy's vision for "landing a man on the moon and returning him safely to the earth" represents:
    ____A. Vision rooted in personal circumstances.
    ____B. Vision rooted in conviction.
    ____C. Vision rooted in a dream.
    ____D. Vision rooted in an idea.

15. Darell Scott's vision is rooted in:
    ____A. An idea.
    ____B. A dream.
    ____C. A personal circumstance.
    ____D. All of the above.

16. Who said "when you pursue noble things, sometimes noble things pursue you?"
    ____A. Robert Kennedy.
    ____B. Bill Bennett.
    ____C. Jack Kemp.
    ____D. John Ashcroft.

17. The workable vision is:
    ____A. A virtuous goal turned into a viable objective.
    ____B. The same thing as the noble vision.
    ____C. Unrelated to the noble vision.
    ____D. Remotely related to the noble vision.

18. The workable vision and the noble vision:
    ____A. Contain built in tensions between the two.
    ____B. Exist as separate but equal.
    ____C. Operate together with little friction.
    ____D. Both B and C.

19. Which of the following is part of implementing the vision?
    ____A. Enlisting others.
    ____B. Motivating others.
    ____C. Overseeing others.
    ____D. All of the above.

20. Finding common ground is part of:
    ____A. Enlisting others.
    ____B. Motivating others.
    ____C. Overseeing others.
    ____D. All of the above.

21. Empowerment is part of:
    ____A. Enlisting others.
    ____B. Motivating others.
    ____C. Overseeing others.
    ____D. All of the above.

22. Acknowledgment is part of:
    ____A. Enlisting others.
    ____B. Motivating others.
    ____C. Overseeing others.
    ____D. None of the above.

23. Communicating purpose and direction is part of:
    ____A. Enlisting others.
    ____B. Motivating others.
    ____C. Overseeing others.
    ____D. All of the above.

24. Empowerment involves:
    ____A. One level where everyone is equally empowered.
    ____B. Various levels where everyone is equally empowered.
    ____C. Various levels that empower some more than others.
    ____D. None of the above.

25. In overseeing others, the leader should remember:
    ____A. That only one style works.
    ____B. That he or she should employ a style that works best for him or her.
    ____C. To use a "hands on" approach.
    ____D. Both A and C.

26. Self-denial is:
    ____A. Consistent with Christian belief.
    ____B. A natural extension of faith.
    ____C. An essential part of serving well.
    ____D. All of the above.

27. According to Attorney Amber Slayton, which of the following traits are most difficult to maintain?
    ____A. Humility and selflessness.
    ____B. Self-sacrifice and selflessness.
    ____C. Self-discipline and selflessness.
    ____D. All of the above.

28. In the context of Chapter Five, a synonym for self-sacrifice is:
    ____A. Humility.
    ____B. Integrity.
    ____C. Love.
    ____D. None of the above.

29. In the context of Chapter Five, a synonym for self-deprecation is:
    ____A. Humility.
    ____B. Integrity.
    ____C. Love.
    ____D. None of the above.

30. U.S.A. Freedom Corps consists of a Board of Directors and is chaired by:
    ____A. The Executive Director for U.S.A. Freedom Corps.
    ____B. The CEO for the Corporation for National and Community Service.
    ____C. The President of the United States.
    ____D. The Vice President of the United States.

31. Which of the following are part of the Corporation for National and Community Service?
    ____A. AmeriCorps.
    ____B. SeniorCorps.
    ____C. Learn and Serve America.
    ____D. All of the above.

32. Which of the following elements may be viewed as a key that unlocks the door to human service?
    ____A. Encouragement.
    ____B. Empathy.
    ____C. Appreciation.
    ____D. Facilitation.

33. Appreciation as an element in service is most related to:
    ____A. Encouragement.
    ____B. Empathy.
    ____C. Facilitation.
    ____D. Respect.

34. A "circle the wagons" mentality implies:
    ____A. A lack of support.
    ____B. A lack of respect.
    ____C. Blanket support all the way down the line of subordinates.
    ____D. A lack of empathy.

35. Which of the following steps—in the process of service—comes first?
    ____A. Desire.
    ____B. Determination.
    ____C. Opportunity.
    ____D. A Plan of Action

36. On what issue has Democrat Tony Hall separated himself from his party?
    ____A. World hunger.
    ____B. Campaign Finance Reform.
    ____C. Pro-life on the issue of abortion.
    ____D. None of the above.

37. What issue represents Tony Hall's passion for serving others?
    ____A. World hunger.
    ____B. National Defense.
    ____C. Taxes.
    ____D. Social Security.

38. Self-renewal in the context of Chapter Seven involves:
    ____A. Personal Wellness.
    ____B. Self Development.
    ____C. Both A and B.
    ____D. Neither A or B.

39. According to Tom Bruno, Jesus did what before he "charged into the battles of life?"
    ____A. He preached and taught on a daily basis.
    ____B. He focused on the physical healing of others.
    ____C. He retreated.
    ____D. He spent time with His disciples.

40. Which of the following examples of Jesus are relevant for the leader's self-renewal?
    ____A. He renewed His faith.
    ____B. He rested.
    ____C. He renewed His mission.
    ____D. All of the above.

41. According to Bruce Bickel and Stan Jantz,
    ____A. Fad diets are worth trying.
    ____B. A healthy body and a sharp mind are unrelated.
    ____C. The focus should be on where you are, rather than where you are going.
    ____D. None of the above.

42. In referencing Mark Twain, what most destructive habit is cited by Bickel and Jantz?
    ____A. A lack of physical fitness.
    ____B. A lack of daily spiritual exercise.
    ____C. Worry.
    ____D. None of the above.

43. In the context of Chapter Eight, credibility is linked to:
    ____A. Upbringing.
    ____B. Character.
    ____C. Accountability.
    ____D. Both B and C.

44. In considering one's credibility in leadership and service, reputation should be viewed:
    ____A. As a side issue.
    ____B. As a major concern.
    ____C. As a permanent concern.
    ____D. As a temporary concern.

45. Which of the following reflect character?
    ____A. Character seeks justice.
    ____B. Character stands up for principle.
    ____C. Character considers others.
    ____D. All of the above.

46. If character is unpretentious, a lack of character
    ____A. Refuses to serve others.
    ____B. Looks out for number one.
    ____C. Is quick to usurp.
    ____D. All of the above.

47. In the context of Chapter Eight, accountability requires:
    ____A. An accountability group.
    ____B. An accountability partner.
    ____C. Holding oneself accountable.
    ____D. All of the above.

48. In explaining why he voted for Articles of Impeachment, Congressman J.C. Watts said he did it for:
    ____A. The voters of his district.
    ____B. The children.
    ____C. The other members of Congress.
    ____D. The executive branch of government.

49. Which of the following is an extension of the Blame Game?
    ____A. The Vilification Game.
    ____B. The Game of Denial.
    ____C. The Prove It Game.
    ____D. The Game of So What?

50. In maintaining character and accountability in service the leader:
    ____A. Helps others.
    ____B. Makes a positive contribution to the cultural environment.
    ____C. Helps secure a personal legacy.
    ____D. All of the above.

Printed in the United States
30447LVS00001B/1-39

9 781591 602163